Anonymous

Pacific Coast Mines and Stock Buyers Manual

How to deal in Stocks

Anonymous

Pacific Coast Mines and Stock Buyers Manual
How to deal in Stocks

ISBN/EAN: 9783744670098

Printed in Europe, USA, Canada, Australia, Japan

Cover: Foto ©ninafisch / pixelio.de

More available books at **www.hansebooks.com**

PACIFIC COAST MINES

—AND—

STOCK BUYER'S MANUAL,

CONTAINING MAP OF COMSTOCK LODE; MAP OF MINING
DISTRICTS ON PACIFIC COAST; SKETCHES OF MINES;
BULLION PRODUCTIONS OF 1875, AND FOR THE
PAST TWENTY-ONE YEARS.

HOW TO DEAL IN STOCKS!

AND A FUND OF VALUABLE INFORMATION.

Entered according to Act of Congress, in the year 1876, by H. M. Van Arnam,
in the Office of the Librarian of Congress.

PRICE ONE DOLLAR.

SAN FRANCISCO:
Francis & Valentine, Commercial Printing House, 517 Clay Street.
1876.

TABLE OF CONTENTS
AND INDEX.

	PAGE.
Pacific Coast Mines and their Productions	3
Trojan Mining Company	5
Atlantic Consolidated Gold and Silver Mine	6
South End, Faught, and DeForest Mines	8
Tahoe, Leviathan, and Cromer Mines	9
Eldorado Silver Mining Co	10
Lee Gold and Silver Mining Co	11
Mining Districts of Nevada and California	12
How to Deal in Mining Stock	14
Morning Star Mining Co	15
Edinburgh Mining Co	16
Hints and Suggestions to Stock Dealers	17
Highest and Lowest of Stock, 1875	18
Silver Sprout Mining Co	19
Virginia Consolidated Mine	20
Electric Mining Co	21
New Coso Mining Co	22
Coso Consolidated Co	23
Pacific Exchange	24
Sunrise Silver Mining Co	38
Sullivan Silver Mining Co	39

STOCK BUYER'S MANUAL.

Introductory	3
S. F. Stock Exchange	5
California Stock Exchange	12
Tabular Statements of Mines	14
Panamint Mining District	27
Cerro Gordo Mining District	36
Calistoga Mine	42

NATIONAL PROSPECTING AND MINING COMPANY.

Principal Office, Merchants' Exchange Building, California Street, San Francisco; Eastern Office, No. —— Chestnut Street, Phila.

This company is an organization for the purpose of buying, selling and locating mining lands and claims. It also organizes mining companies, places the stock, and attends to the erection of mills and furnaces upon mines already discovered. The company extends its operations throughout the entire mining regions of the Pacific Coast, and will have branch offices in all the principal cities of the United States and Europe. Specimens of ores of the precious metals can be seen at their offices, and full information obtained in regard to the mineral products of the most valuable mining districts in the United States. This company is organized under the most flattering auspices, the officers being well-known gentlemen of ability, and those at all interested in mines or minerals should not fail to give them a call.

WM. H. WILCOX, President. JOHN W. MORRIS, Vice-Prest.
T. LATHAM WISWALL, Sec'y. H. H. HOBBS, Treasurer.

Directors.

WM. H. WILLCOX,   JOHN W. MORRIS,
T. LATHAM WISWALL,   HIRAM H. HOBBS,
WALTER J. WELCH,   GEORGE T. TRUMAN.
         WM. R. ARMSTRONG.

LAFAYETTE E. SEAMAN, General Manager.

CHARLES E. CONVIS, Stock and Money Broker, No. 9 Halleck's Building. Take Elevator to Third Floor.

PACIFIC COAST MINES AND THEIR PRODUCTIONS.

When gold was first discovered in California, those who flocked to this beautiful State were content to confine their researches for the precious metal on the river bars, or along the beds of creeks, and in gulches among the Sierras. Thousands of dollars were thus gathered, and no one of the hardy miners ever dreamed of the immense quartz-lodes of gold and silver which lay far down in the bowels of the rock-ribbed mountains. Time passed on, and the far-seeing speculators, after learning that ore-croppings had been seen on the sides of lofty mountains, commenced sinking shafts on these croppings, and met with so much success that quartz-mining became the rule, and gravel or placer-mining the exception. There are, however, many claims worked by hydraulic means, which pay largely. The silver deposits which underlie Mount Davidson, in Nevada, were discovered in 1858, and a great excitement was caused thereby, which resulted in the formation of a new State, and the adding of millions of dollars to the wealth of the world. Such mines as the Gould and Curry, Ophir, and others well known to the world yielded bullion way up into the millions; but the wildest dreamer never for a moment imagined that such vast ore bodies existed as has since been found in the mines known as the Consolidated Virginia and California. The extraordinary depths at which ore was found in these mines, caused other mine owners to sink deep on theirs, and the year 1876 will see such vast ore bodies uncovered as will far exceed the wildest dreams of the most enthusiastic.

In 1875, the following ore was produced from the various mining States and Territories:

Nevada,	$40,000,000
California,	20,000,000
Oregon,	1,200,000
Washington Territory	100,000
Idaho	2,000,000
Montana,	3,500,000
Utah,	6,000,000
Colorado,	9,000,000
New Mexico and Arizona	100,000

In addition to the above, British Columbia made a production of about $2,000,000, and Lower California about $500,000, most of which came to San Francisco for coinage or shipment abroad. About $1,500,000 in bullion reached the city from the northwestern coast of Mexico in 1875. It will thus be seen that the entire production of our Pacific Coast mines for 1875 will fall little short of $100,000,000, and the production from 1845 to 1875, inclusive, amounts to the enormous sum of $1,584,040,000, of which $265,781,400 was in silver, and the remainder in gold.

New mines are daily being discovered, and the Panamint and Cerro Gordo districts in California, a notice of which will be found under the proper heading in this book, will be opened up largely.

In their proper order will be found sketches of leading mines in Nevada and California, to which the capitalist and all who are interested in mines can pay their attention with profit. Wherever a ledge appears, and the work is prosecuted with vigor, no one need be afraid but that paying ore will be obtained; hence it is idle to attempt to point out which mine is likely to first pay a dividend. In 1873, stock of the Consolidated Virginia sold at $3 and $5 per share. In 1875, in January it brought $800 per share, and to-day, April 1876, some of those who own shares receive dividends to the amount of $1,000,000 *per month*.

The aggregate sales of mining stock in the San Francisco Stock and Exchange Board, in 1875, was $220,222,890.

The entire product of ore from the Consolidated Virginia, in 1875, was $18,000,000, and altogether, over $30,000,000 have been produced from that mine alone, and there is in sight in that mine and the California, $170,000,000. Every county in Nevada is ore-producing, and no county in California can be found without some productions in the precious metals. A list of districts will be found under the proper heading.

THE TROJAN MINING COMPANY.

This mine is located in Gold Hill District, on the Comstock belt of mines, and lies west of the Overman and east of Reliance. It is one of the oldest locations, having been worked in the early days of mining, as the Gold dust and Trojan ore from this mine in those times paid over $30 a ton, and, although at that time not profitable, is largely so now on account of the present facilities and advantages for milling and mining.

PROGRESS OF DEVELOPMENT.

Work on the mine is being prosecuted with vigor. The depth of the shaft, which is a double 4x4½ feet in the clear, is now, April, 1876, nearly 200 feet. At a distance of 80 feet from the surface, the shaft passed through a fine vein of ore, eight feet in thickness, pitching to the eastward; a drift was then run 60 feet to the westward, at which point another ledge, eight feet in thickness, was struck. The shaft was then continued down to the level of the 187-foot level, at which point a drift was run 190 feet to the westward, passing through two other ore bodies, one—eight, and the other twelve feet in thickness. A winze was then started on the ore vein west of the shaft, on the 60-foot level, and sunk to the level of the 187-foot drift, passing through ore the entire distance. There has been no difficulty in disposing of the stock of this company for working capital, as it was very active, and a large fund has been raised for the full development of the mine. The company have unbounded confidence in the great value of this property, and have erected hoisting works capable of sinking 1000 feet or more. The number of feet in the mine is 1,500; capital stock $10,000,000, divided into 100,000 shares. Location of office, 328 Montgomery Street, room 22.

JAMES J. GREEN, President.   WM. JAY SMITH, Vice-Prest.
DAVID WILDER, Secretary.

Directors.

JAMES J. GREEN,   WM. JAY SMITH,
CHAS. E. PEARSON,   JOHN W. ROWE,
PATRICK CONNOLLY.

THE ATLANTIC CONSOLIDATED GOLD AND SILVER MINE.

This mine is located about one mile west of Silver City, but a short distance south of Justice, the main entrances to its developments being on the south bank of the American Ravine, and is the acknowledged king of its district. [We quote from the *Daily Mining Reporter*, Silver City, Nev., Tuesday, March 14, 1876.]—ED.

ITS OLD DEVELOPMENTS,

Made from '61 to '63, and from which nearly three-quarters of a million of dollars were taken out, consist of a main shaft and three tunnels or levels put in at the respective distances of 120, 220, and 320 feet. The first is in 180, the second 275, and the third 386 feet. An average of fifteen feet of ore, that milled in the Brooks, Franklin and Swansea mills from $38 to $40 per ton, was taken out of these three tunnels. These results were gained by the old Atlantic Company, whose operations were suspended in August, 1863. With the exception of a large quantity of ore taken out of a winze in the 320-foot level, and worked at a profit by the Rigby brothers in 1864, nothing more was done in the mine until December, 1875, at which time the developments of the Atlantic Consolidated Mining Company—

THE PRESENT COMPANY—

Were commenced. This company is composed principally of English capitalists from London, joined by men of equal financial prominence in San Francisco, and some of the original owners of the mine. J. W. Brown, Esq., a thorough business man, and one having a large and most successful experience in the direction and superintendence of mines on the Pacific coast, has been put in charge and commenced

THE NEW DEVELOPMENTS

by driving in a 420-foot level from the surface. This level commences from the bed of the ravine, and is now pushed into the mine and ore body a distance of 620 feet. Five hundred and thirty feet from the entrance a cross-cut of thirty-five feet has been made to the east, and has exposed a solid body of ore thirty feet in width, from which not one pound can be taken that will not pay for milling, and from which assays of from

$30 TO $100 PER TON

Have been obtained. This cross-cut is the junction of the twin veins—or, more properly speaking, the white and red ledges—and presents the finest body of ore that can be found outside of the Consolidated Virginia. The red ledge, which comes in from the southeast, has a preponderance of gold, and at the second cross-cut carries full thirteen feet of ore that will average $120 per ton. This cross-cutting and the driving in of the 420-foot level is the present base of operations, and it is from this point the entire mine will be put in working condition. In this, as in the levels above, a solid body of valuable mineral presents itself at every turn of the explorer, and one finds himself more agreeably astonished as he stops to more closely inspect the compact mass with the prospecting glass. There is an unbroken body of not less than 186 feet of rich ore between the 320 and 420-foot levels,

A MASS OF MINERAL IN SIGHT,

The value of which it would be difficult to estimate. In the Atlantic, as in the monarch ledge of the Comstock, one gets a proper idea of what is meant by the expression, "millions of dollars in sight," for there, certainly, is the gigantic mass of money, in crude condition, only waiting the pick of the miner, the clank of the stamps, and the heat of the furnace to convert it into glittering coin. This is no manufacture of reportorial imagination. The mine is open to the public, the mineral is there in quantities that will astonish all who visit it, and the most careful experiments will more than verify our statements.

For nearly ten years the lower level of this mine supplied Silver City and some of our mills with an abundant supply of water, and was uninhabitable for a working force; but when the Overman mine cut its present body of water she tapped the main artery which kept the Atlantic flooded, and has now left the latter mine perfectly dry, and enabled its working to be prosecuted. This water find of

THE OVERMAN SIMPLY DRAINS THE ATLANTIC

To a depth of 1,100 feet, and has conferred a direct benefit, gratis, that would have cost many thousand dollars to have obtained.

From the 320 to the 420-foot level a shaft was sunk in early days, and on cutting the clay on the east a body of water was tapped, which so suddenly flooded the shaft that the miners escaped drowning only by leaving all tools and being speedily drawn to the top. The Overman, having now drained the mine, ample hoisting works, provided with a double-cylinder engine, will be soon placed at this shaft to assist in

EXTRACTING THE ORE,

Which it will strike about 500 feet from the 320-foot level. It will be seen from this what complete preparations are being made to work the mine systematically, and with force enough to employ all the mills. No one who visits the mine will doubt for a moment that such preparations are fully justified and are required to work the mine as it should be to make it a paying mine from the start. There are 3,300 feet in the Atlantic, United States patented location, and the stock has been divided into

ONE HUNDRED THOUSAND SHARES.

Par value of $100 each, making capital stock $10,000,000.

Directors.

CHAS. H. AITKEN, President.   J. BARR ROBERTSON.
JESSE W. BROWN.   CHARLES JONES,

PETER ROBERTSON, Secretary, office Academy Building, 330 Pine street.

SOUTH END MINING COMPANY.

The property of this company is situated about 2,200 feet south of the "Silver Hill" mine and about half a mile west of Silver City. Its dimensions are 1,500 feet north and south by 600 feet in width, title perfect. It was incorporated February 25th, 1876, by E. F. Stone, J. M. Walker, W. T. Lyle, John Skae and R. N. Graves, with a capital of $10,000,000.

DESCRIPTION.

The mine has two distinct ledges, the west ledge being the same as that found in the "Justice," while the east vein is gold-bearing, and has the characteristics of the gold and silver veins of Batapilas District in Mexico.

The company is now sinking a durable compartment shaft, some forty feet east of the east wall of their west vein, while they are also driving an incline on the east vein. The quartz, so far as has been tested, assays from $15 to $400 per ton, in gold and silver. It is the intention of the company to place machinery on at once for sinking 1,000 feet. It is the opinion of all who have examined this mine that it will justify most any expenditure of capital, for it is undoubtedly on the true Comstock vein, and will require but little time and a small expenditure to develop it into a dividend-paying mine.

Office, 418 California Street, Room No. 2; Dr. J. W. Clark, Secretary; Col. W. T. Robinson, Superintendent.

THE FAUGHT MINE

Is located east of the "Atlantic Consolidated," and on the east extension of the east vein of the South End Mine. Still to be incorporated and developed, but no doubt exists as to its ultimate importance. The locator and owner is W. F. Faught.

THE DeFOREST MINE

Adjoins the "South End," and is undoubtedly on the same vein. Col. W. T. Robinson is the locator and present owner.

CROMER MINE.

This mine is located in the Devil's Gate District, in Lyon County, Nevada. It was located in January, 1875, on a true ledge, and work is now progressing rapidly in its development. There has been taken out of the shaft, which is 200 feet deep, about 200 tons of ore which showed, upon being assayed, a very high grade. The ore is getting richer as more developments are being made, and there is no doubt but what this will prove, in a very brief time, a good dividend-paying mine.

The Trustees are N. ATKINSON, R. Y. SNOWBALL, H. A. DEMING, GEORGE BENSON, and J. E. JEWELL.

President, H. A. DEMING.
Secretary, T. E. LUTY.
Superintendent, JASPER BABCOCK.

Office, 507 Montgomery Street, Room A, San Francisco.

LEVIATHAN.

This mine was located on the Comstock Lode, in 1863, but was not incorporated until 1874. The developments which were made in neighboring mines gave assurance to the proprietors of the Leviathan of there being very rich ore in their mine. Work has been, and is still being pushed vigorously, and the shaft is 600 feet deep. Ore has been found which assays at a very high grade, and the prospects for developing a dividend-paying mine are most flattering. There is 2,000 feet in the mine. Number of shares 100,000.

Office 507 Montgomery Street, San Francisco.

Directors.

W. H. PATTERSON.   FRANK CICOTT.   N. ATKINSON.
T. E. JEWELL.   JOEL BALL.

W. H. PATTERSON, President.
F. E. LUTY, Sec'y.   JASPER BABCOCK, Sup't.

TAHOE MINE.

This mine is located adjoining the south line of the "Lady Bryan," in what is known as the Flowery District, Storey County, Nevada. It is in a direct southeast line from the Ophir mine, in which the ore body is running directly toward the Tahoe and Lady Bryan. The Tahoe has a claim 1200 feet wide and 1500 feet long. The company has organized with a capital stock of $10,000,000, divided into 100,000 shares. The Daily Stock Report, of March 30, says, in regard to this mine:

"The Tahoe Mining Company, lately incorporated to mine in Storey County, Nevada, have purchased mining ground adjoining the south line of the Lady Bryan, 1500 feet long and 1200 feet wide. The explorations being made on the Lady Bryan are within a few hundred feet of their south line, indicating a strong vein over 150 feet in width and a constant improvement in quality of ore, and affording perfect drainage and ventilation, thereby giving an opportunity to develop the Tahoe mine at a great saving in cost of machinery and pumping which otherwise could not have been avoided. Work will be prosecuted at the mine as soon as material can be delivered. Machinery will be placed in position with power to sink the shaft to a depth of 1,000 feet. Samples of ore at the Company's office, 507 Montgomery street, room 3, show an abundance of silver sulphurets, and promise well for future developments soon to be made."

Directors.

GEORGE BENSON, President.   J. F. NESBIT.
NATHAN ATKINSON, Vice Prest.   T. E. JEWELL.
MARTIN JONES.

F. E. LUTY, Secretary, 507 Montgomery St., Room "A," San Francisco.

ELDORADO SILVER MINING COMPANY, LOWER CALIFORNIA.

This mine is located about sixty-five miles south of San Diego, and six miles from the Bay of Encinata. The bay has deep water to the wharf. Encinata is a port of entry. There is a good wagon road from the wharf to the mine. The Company is incorporated at nearly half the usual rate, viz: 52,480 shares at the nominal par price of $100 per share. The secretary is Mr. J. J. Tobin, of the firm of Vernon, Tobin & Co., on Montgomery street, in the Safe Deposit building. It is mainly a proprietory mine, so that the stock is not on the market.

It is well known to mining experts that these Lower California mines are reeking with wealth, but capitalists hesitate to further their development until they have the guarantee of the Stars and Stripes. At the same time, it is to be borne in mind that the probably imminent raising of that flag will increase the value of genuine property in Lower California tenfold.

We have ourselves seen *bulk* assays from this mine running over $300, made by Huhn & Luckhardt, First street—and this before the mother ledge was cut by the Company's tunnel (they have now cut the ledge); so that we may safely calculate on draining, in the interest of our California capitalists, some of the undeveloped wealth of our sleepy sister, Mexico.

LEE GOLD AND SILVER MINING COMPANY.

This mine is located on the Comstock Lode, and extends fifteen hundred feet north and south on the ledge. It is situated due south of the Consolidated Virginia, and north of Justice; is due east of and adjoins New York Consolidated; west of Alta, adjoining Lady Washington on the north. The New York Consolidated has a shaft 800 feet deep, and from indications bids fair to be a rich mine. The Lee promises to equal or excel the New York Consolidated.

The ledge shows conclusively a contact vein, running north and south, with good croppings; and there is no doubt but that it will prove, upon further development, to be rich in deposits of the precious metals.

EXTENT OF WORK DONE.

A new shaft is being sunk, and has attained a depth of 100 feet (April 1st, 1876), with the most favorable indications, the ore assaying $50 per ton. The Alta, which adjoins the Lee on the west, has sunk a shaft about 400 feet. Justice, at the 450-foot level, and also at the 800-foot level, had very rich ore, and in large quantities, and the Lee will undoubtedly find rich ore at the 400-foot level.

The number of feet in the mine is 1,500; number of shares 100,000.

Trustees.

H. H. HOBBS, JOHN TREADWELL,
J. M. SEAMENS, J. W. MOYLE,
R. W. HAMILTON.

H. H. HOBBS, President.

C. J. EATON, Secretary, office 402 Montgomery Street, room 7, San Francisco, Cal.

Below will be found a partial list of the mining districts in Nevada and California. Those of Nevada are given first.

STOREY COUNTY.

American Flat,	Flowery,	North Virginia,
Virginia' City.		

LYON COUNTY.

Devil's Gate,	Silver City,	Chinatown.

ELKO COUNTY.

Bald Mountain,	Bull Run,	Centennial,
Cornucopia,	Delano,	Grand Junction,
Hick's City,	Island Mountain,	Kit Carson,
Kensley,	Lucine,	Mineral Hill,
Marseilles,	Racine,	Railroad,
Salmon River,	Silver Zone,	Tuscarora,
Wyoming.		

LANDER COUNTY.

Augusta,	Battle Mountain,	Big Creek,
Bunker Hill,	Bullion,	Grass Valley,
Lewis,	Mount Hope,	Ravenswood,
Reese River,	Roberts,	Santa Fe,
Simpson Park,	Summit.	

NYE COUNTY.

Danville,	Empire,	Bryant,
Hot Creek,	Jefferson,	Lodi,
Mammoth,	Monitor,	Morey,
Manhattan,	Milk Spring,	North Union,
Ophir Cañon,	Park Cañon,	Reveille,
Spanish Belt,	Silver Cloud,	Silver Point,
Seneca,	San Antonia,	St. Clair,
Springfield,	St. Elmo,	Troy,
Tybo,	Washington,	Union.

WHITE PINE COUNTY.

Antelope,	Cherry Creek,	Cooper,
Egan,	Hunter,	Hercules,
Lake,	Nevada,	Pinto,
Robinson,	Ruby Hill,	Shell Creek,
Sacramento,	San Francisco,	Taylor,
White Pine,	Ward,	Suake,
Shoshone,	Washoe County,	Galena,
Peavine,	Washoe.	

PIOCHE COUNTY.

Bristol,	Cave,	Chief,
Groom,	Highland,	Pahmagat,
Patterson,	Pennyslvania,	Silver Park.

Some of the principal Mining Districts of California:

SHASTA COUNTY.

Buckeye,	Bear Creek,	Dog Creek,
French Gulch,	Horse Town,	Muletown,
Middletown,	North Cow Creek,	Pittsburg,
Shasta,	South Fork,	Whiskeytown.

LASSEN COUNTY.

Coppervale,	Crœsus,	Diamond Mountain,
Hayden Hill,	Richmond.	

SIERRA COUNTY.

Alleghany,	Brandy City,	Downieville,
Eureka,	Gibsonville,	Harland Flat,
Indian Hill,	Forest City,	Plum Valley,
Potosi,	Port Wine,	Minnesota,
Monte Cristo,	Morristown,	Newark,
St. Louis,	Scales.	

TUOLUMNE COUNTY.
Tuolumne District.

PLUMAS COUNTY.

Buck Ranch,	Caraboo,	Cherokee,
Cascade,	Duch Hill,	Elizabethtown,
Genessee,	Indian Valley,	Jamison Creek,
Laporte,	Light Cañon,	Mount Pleasant,
Mohawk,	Marion Flat,	Nelson Creek,
Quartz,	Round Valley,	Rich Bar,
Richmond Hill,	Spanish Ranch,	Saw Pit,
Union Flat.		

COLUSA COUNTY.

Sulphur Creek, Yolo County Mining District.

SAN BERNARDINO COUNTY.

Clark,	Holcomb Valley,	Lone Valley,
Bear Valley,	Lytle Creek,	Twenty-nine Palms,
Resting Springs,	Mohave,	Liberal,
Cucumonga,	Lane,	Temescal,
Swarthout,	Riverside,	Whitewater,
Ord,	San Bernardino,	Ava Watts,
Bitter Springs,	Macedonia.	

ALPINE COUNTY.

Alpine, Monitor, Silver Mountain.

INYO COUNTY.

Cerro Gordo,	Coso,	Panamint,
Owens' Lake.		

HOW TO DEAL IN MINING STOCKS.

Those unacquainted with the *modus operandi* of stock-dealing can soon learn all about it by a little practical experience, but, as a starter, we will say to them, you can buy through any responsible broker to the extent of your purse, and can buy regular, or 10, 20, or 30. For instance: You go to a broker, and give an order for him to buy you 100 shares of California at, say, $100 per share; if you buy regular this will cost you $10,000; if you only want to speculate, you will have him *carry* 100 shares for you for an indefinite time, and will pay him from 30 to 50 per cent. of the par value of the stock; but should the stock depreciate in value, your broker will call for more money to make your margin good—this is called "putting up more mud." You can buy at 10, 20, or 30 days, by putting up from 30 to 50 per cent., and can call for the stock at any time within your time specified in the contract; the seller, however, has no right to deliver the stock until the expiration of the full time. The commission of the broker is usually from ½ to 1 per cent.

California Mines.

	FEET.	SHARES.
Booth,	1,850	40,000
WASHOE.		
Amazon Consolidated,	1,500	30,000
Baltic Consolidated,	2,100	37,000
Bonanza,	1,140	10,000
Cramer,	1,500	100,000
Glasgow,	1,500	60,000
Jacob Little Consolidated	3,280	100,000
Leviathan,	2,000	100,000
Maryland,	900	54,000
Monumental,	1,500	90,000
Morning Star,	1,600	80,000
North Consolidated Virginia,	1,500	100,000
Original Flowery,	1,000	50,000
Pioneer Consolidated,	1,500	100,000
Prospect,	1,000	100,000
Scorpion,	4,000	40,000
Trojan,	1,700	100,000
WHITE PINE.		
General Lee,	1,000	20,000
Geneva Consolidated,	3,000	50,000
Ward Ellis,	2,000	40,000
IDAHO.		
Pauper,	1,600	50,000
South Mountain,		1,600
MISCELLANEOUS.		
Tybo Consolidated,		50,000
Advance,	1,200	100,000
New Almaden,	10,000	200,000
Cose Consolidated,	4,500	10,000

NOTE.—Mining Companies, the stock of which has been increased since the tables were printed: Andes, from 50,000 to 100,000 shares. Justice to 105,000. Exchequer, to 100,000. Savage, to 112,000. Consolidated Virginia, to 540,000. Yellow Jacket, to 112,000. Lady Washington, from 30,000 to 60,000.

MORNING STAR.

This mine is located on the Comstock Lode, between the Sierra Nevada and Utah, and contains sixteen hundred (1,600) lineal feet on the vein. It was located in the year 1860.

A tunnel has been run and cut the ledge, which is the Red Ledge or Bonanza, at the depth of 300 feet from the surface. The width of the ledge is thirty-two feet, and the ore pulped fifty dollars per ton.

There is now a three-compartment working shaft being sunk, and at a depth of 600 feet will drift for the ledge.

The location is one of the best on the Comstock, and the owners intend working it to the best advantage of all parties interested.

The mine was incorporated in April, 1875, with a perfect title, and is free from debt.

The Directors have concluded to place 25,000 shares for Working Capital, which, they are satisfied, will pay all expenses incurred in reaching the ledge.

TOTAL NUMBER OF SHARES, 30,000.

DIRECTORS.—Martin White, John Martin, Peter Mathews, G. E. Clark, J. A. Hunt. President Martin White; Secretary, George E. Grimes; Superintendent, John R. Logan.

Office, Room No. 7, STEVENSON BLOCK, cor. California and Montgomery Streets.

THE EDINBURGH MINE.

This Mine is situated in the Devil's Gate Mining District, Lyon County, Nevada, and was located in the year 1863, and was worked for gold only. Work was then suspended, and was not resumed until 1875, when a company was formed, and incorporated August 9th, of the same year. The Company is known as the EDINBURGH GOLD AND SILVER MINING COMPANY, and composed of the following named managers:

Dr. S. J. Corbett, Hon. J. J. Owen, J. H. Adams, S. J. Lewis, M. S. Wadsworth. Dr. S. J. Corbett, President; R. P. Hosmer, Secretary.

The property is divided into 60,000 shares, at a par value of $100 per share. 20,000 shares are set aside for a working capital. Work is now in progress on the mine. A fine double-compartment shaft was commenced 300 feet East of the croppings, and, at the present date, has a depth of 100 feet; thoroughly timbered throughout.

The vein has a N. E. and S. W. course, and joins the Amazon Consolidated Mine on the North. The ledge dips at an angle of 41 degrees, and shows a true fissure vein, at an average width of fifteen feet between casings. The mine consists of 1,500 linear feet, with 300 feet each side of ledge. The Silver City branch of the Virginia and Truckee Railroad passes within 300 feet of the mine, where all supplies for the mine are delivered.

The future of the mine looks very flattering, and, for location and geological formation, there is nothing South of the Belcher, yet discovered, that bids so fair to become one of our prominent paying mines as THE EDINBURGH.

LEVIATHAN MINING COMPANY,

OFFICE:—507 Montgomery Street, S. F.

DIRECTORS.

W. H. PATTERSON, FRANK X. CICOTT, N. ATKINSON,
T. E. JEWELL, JOEL BALL.
PRESIDENT.—W. H. PATTERSON.   SECRETARY.—F. E. LUTY
SUPERINTENDENT.—JASPER BABCOCK.

HINTS AND SUGGESTIONS TO THOSE DEALING IN STOCKS.

The business of stock dealing is one which has assumed such vast proportions in San Francisco and other localities on the Pacific Coast, that it can be safely said seven out of ten of the business men are now, or have been at times, more or less interested in this business; and people in every walk of life watch the fluctuations of the stock market with the most intense eagerness.

It may be proper, therefore, to give here some hints to stock buyers that may be useful to them.

FIRST.—To the uninitiated we would say: When you have made up your mind to buy stocks select the ones you have the most confidence in. Ascertain the history of the mine; its location; the extent of the ledge; its probable durability; the character and quality of the ore it produces; the number of feet and number of shares in the mine; how often the shares have been increased, if at all; the number of assessments and number of dividends, if any. Then ascertain in whose hands the management of the mine is; are the directors men of character and honesty, for much depends upon the honesty of these directors, presidents and secretaries. As rich strikes are always purely matters of chance, no one can conjecture what mine will be the next to strike a bonanza. It may, however, be said, that some mines are worked on a certainty of "striking it rich." Watch the market carefully, and sell out at a reasonable advance, and do not wait for too great a rise. The most successful stock operators on California Street are those who have been content with fair profits. It is better to sell on a declining market, if by so doing you can realize anything. For instance, if you are holding Ophir, and the market declines 25 per cent., and by selling you can realize 25 per cent. on your investment, do so; and by buying again when the market is low, you can realize both ways.

Stock speculation is not gambling, but a science, and by following these general rules you will rarely fail of being successful in your ventures.

THE DAILY STOCK REPORT should be read each day carefully, and it may be regarded as standard authority on all questions relating to stocks, prices, fluctuations, assessments, dividends, etc., as this paper has unusual facilities for obtaining news.—One of its proprietors is the secretary of the S. F. Stock Board, and its leading editor is Mr. Wm. M. Bunker,—both live men. Everyone should read the paper that is at all interested in stocks.

Below will be found the fluctuations of some of the leading stocks dealt in in this city. The price is given for January, 1875, and December of the same year.

	JAN. 1875.	DEC.
Con. Virginia	$700	$360
*California	780	63½
Chollar Potosi	95	112
Caledonia	37	26½–16
Belcher	57½	27
Best & Belcher	89	52½
Confidence	59	17
Crown Point	47½	25
Hale & Norcross	79	35
*Justice	180	23¾
*Julia	25	14
Kentuck	26	13½
Knickerbocker	7½	1½
Kossuth	5¼	2¾
Lady Bryan	13	1½
Lady Washington	5	2½
Leopard	—	12½
Leviathan	3½	1¼
Mexican	85	18¼
Morning Star	—	4¾
New York	7½	1⅞
Ophir	315	42½
Overman	99	53
Phil Sheridan	7	½
*Rock Island	15	3¼
Savage	190	12
Seg. Belcher	165	80
Sierra Nevada	27	16¼
Silver Hill	18	7½
Succor	9	½
Union Con	95	8¾
Yellow Jacket	174	82

Those marked with an * the stock has been increased; those in California, five for one.

SILVER SPROUT MINING CO.

The property of this company is located in Kearsarge Mining District, Inyo County, California, and within eight miles of the terminus of the Independence and Los Angeles Railroad, and consists of some fifteen different lodes,—the two most valuable being the Silver Sprout and Lamb. The Silver Sprout is a well defined vein, carrying both gold and silver, and varying in width from three to nine feet. It is now opened to a depth of one hundred feet, and work is still being prosecuted. A more perfect fissure has never been found, the famous Comstock not excepted.

Ore from this mine has been shipped to San Francisco, which yielded from ONE HUNDRED AND FIFTY TO SEVEN HUNDRED AND TWENTY DOLLARS per ton, giving evidence that the mine will afford any amount of ore that will yield from $50 to $250 per ton. The Lamb lode is also a well-defined lead varying from three to six feet, carrying both gold and silver, and affording a large amount of milling ore, that will yield from $50 to $100 per ton. These two mines are five hundred and fifty feet apart and between them are some thirteen veins, varying in width from six inches to three feet, all carrying ore of equal richness with the two main veins. It is quite evident, that at a great depth this entire cluster to which the company have undisputed title, concentrates and forms ore deposit of fabulous value. This cluster is located at an altitude of about 10,000 feet above the ocean, in the main belt of the Sierra Nevadas, and will compare well with the most valuable mines of Mexico, the most prolific of which are at similar altitudes.

THE FACILITIES FOR WORKING THESE MINES

Are unequalled, as the lodes cut the mountains nearly at right angles, so a tunnel 1,000 feet in length would give from 750 to 1,000 feet depth on the mine; and where it takes half a million of dollars to gain a depth of 1,000 feet on the Comstock, less than $25,000 will accomplish the same result here.

AMPLE WATER POWER

Is at hand for reduction of the ores. There never has been any conflicting title to the property, and all legal steps have been taken for securing a U. S. Patent. There is no mining stock which presents such a prospect of great value.

The stock is divided into 50,000 shares of $100 par value each.

Directors.

NATHANIEL PAGE, President. ALMARIN B. PAUL.
B. F. TUTTLE. GEORGE HEARST.
A. WINGARD.
T. B. WINGARD, Sec'y, Office, 318 California street.

VIRGINIA CONSOLIDATED MINING CO.

This company's property is situated in Kearsarge Mining District, Inyo County, California, and comprises a cluster of veins known as the Virginia.

The Virginia is the main vein and into which all the others give evidence of emerging. Developments on the Virginia mine are by a shaft 120 feet deep, and a tunnel of 200 feet in length, which shows a well defined lead six feet in width.

THE ORE CONTAINS BOTH SILVER AND GOLD,

And assays from $50 to $689 per ton. The most of the assays going from $200 to $300 per ton. The ore is of good milling character and carries a larger percentage of gold than any mine in the district has yet developed.

THE FACILITIES FOR MINING

And reducing ores is without a parallel, and which greatly enhances the value of mining property. Here great depths can be gained by comparatively short tunnels. Water power is ample for reducing works of any reasonable capacity. The company own both water rights and mill sites, and expect soon to have the mines sufficiently opened to justify the erection of suitable works.

This section of country is now attracting a great deal of attention, and no district presents such a show of rich milling ores as are to be found in the range of mountains in which the Virginia is situated, they being in the main belt of the Sierra Nevadas. The altitude of these mines is about 9,000 feet above the ocean, at the same time are easy of access and ores can be cheaply transmitted by tramway to works at the base. This stock is divided into 60,000 shares of $100 par value each. This Company owns 10,000 shares of reserved stock which will be disposed of (if required when the present capital is exhausted,) at a reasonable figure, to be used as a working capital, thereby avoiding the necessity of assessments.

Directors.

ROBERT P. CHASE, President.   JOHN MALLON.
A. F. BERNARD.   EUGENE CHENOT.
J. F. CARROLL.
T. B. WINGARD, Secretary, 318 California street.

ELECTRIC MINING COMPANY.

The location of the mining and milling property of the Electric Mining Company is situated in Lincoln Mining District, Butte County, Cal., about thirteen miles from the city of Oroville, and two miles from the town of Enterprise.

The Company's reduction Works are situated two miles from Enterprise, or three miles from Forbestown, on the north shore of the South Fork of Feather river. The Quartz mill is a dry crusher, with drying furnace, stamp, battery, barrels, and all the machinery necessary for working the ores by Paul's dry reducing and dry amalgamating process, and arranged to work automatically as soon as ore leaves the furnace. The power used is water, supplied from the Mooretown Ditch Company, and the reducing capacity, as standing at present, from eight to ten tons per day of twenty-four hours.

The Company owns a water right on the South Fork of the Feather river, situated about half a mile above the quartz mill, where, by the erection of a mill-dam and flume, sufficient water can be brought to the mill for a reducing power of from fifty to one hundred tons per day.

At present the principal and best developed mine is the Mammoth, situated on the south side of the above-mentioned river, and connected with the mill by a substantial bridge, high enough above high water mark to insure its safety, and by a car track along the shore of the river of about one-fourth of a mile in length, which enables the Company to deliver their ore from the mine at only a nominal expense, and with no second handling after the same leaves the ore stopes.

This claim is a series of a number of veins, and the croppings of the two most promising ledges are near the extreme northwestern boundary, about two hundred feet above the level of the river; and while continuing explorations along the vein to its southeastern boundary, a depth of from 700 to 800 feet can be obtained, above water level of the river. Only a short distance from the southeastern boundary the croppings of one of the mines appears about eight feet thick, and resembles the favorable character of the ore of the vein most developed.

A tunnel of seventy-five feet in length, eighty feet down from the croppings, has been run to intersect the vein at right angles, and which was found to measure about two feet in thickness, very regular in its course, and having perfect walls and white clay selvages to indicate the vein to be a true ledge. At the southeastern end of its course in the drift, it appears to be widening. A level of fifty to sixty feet in length has been run on the vein, and the ore appears very uniform in its character. Free gold, and decomposed iron sulphurets richly charged with gold, seem to be the only metals present.

The next vein of this series is situated about thirty feet higher up the hill, and on a level only about twenty feet distant from the first described one, and running parallel with the same. By extending the tunnel, both veins can be worked by the same, and gaining the advantage of ventilation from each other. The mine is dry, and no heavy outlay necessary for timbering for a number of years. The ore of this second vein appears even more favorable than that of the first, and shows in addition other metals, such as carbonate of copper and sulphate of lead—always considered a good feature, in gold mining, for continuation of metal.

The mountain-spur on which these veins appear runs up the so-called Forbestown ridge. Veins appear to crop out all along the same, some of which are undoubtedly extensions of the Mammoth series of ledges. A tunnel of one hundred feet in length has been run on one of the veins nearest to the river and only a little above high-water mark, this vein showing an average thickness of one foot, but very heavily charged with gold-bearing sulphurets.

As far as this claim is developed it shows a large amount of ore in prospect, of a character to prove not only paying but also remunerative to the stockholders. Capital stock, $2,500,000; 50,000 shares at $50 a share.

Directors.

Geo. McDonald.
W. Seawell,
S. D. Woods.
Almarin B. Paul.
C. W. Clayes.
T. B. Wingard.
G. W. Haskell.

STOCK BROKERS.

Coll. Deane, Pres. S. F. Stock Exchange, 309 California Street.

Harris & Hart, 321 California Street.

Marshall, Seth & Co., 311 California Street.

A. C. Taylor, 411½ California Street.

Linderman & Taylor, cor. Pine and Montgomery Sts.

NEW COSO MINING COMPANY.

The new Coso Mining Company is operating in the New Coso Mining District, Inyo County, State of California, where it owns the Christmas Gift and Lucky Jim mines, and a one-half interest in the Cuervo Springs. The New Coso District comprises a large number of argentiferous galena mines, some of which like the Defiance, Christmas Gift and Lucky Jim mines, have been opened up to an extent showing permanent values.

Office, 318 California street, San Francisco, Cal.

From the mines of the New Coso Company there had been extracted up to the 1st of August, some 1,500 tons of first-class ore, averaging $125 per ton. There had been sunk five shafts, and these 1,500 tons were obtained in sinking these shafts. Since then stoping has been commenced and the mines are daily furnishing some seventy-five tons. The Company has, at a cost of $50,000, erected two first-class furnaces, having a capacity of seventy-five tons per day. These furnaces are situated some three miles from the Company's mines, on an easy down grade. Wood and water are at convenient distances, and the furnaces are supplied with both at reasonable figures. The furnaces started up on Monday, August 16th, the ores swelling like "peas." The Directors of the Company are: L. L. Robinson, President; G. D. Roberts, W. H. V. Cronise, George W. Kidd and J. W. Gashwiler. Secretary, D. F. Verdenal; Treasurer, Merchants' Exchange Bank; and Superintendent, C. E. Hoffman. There are 100,000 shares in the company. Location of office, 409 California street, San Francisco.

THE COSO CONSOLIDATED MINING CO.

In the Spring of 1875, the "Bella Union," "Raleigh," "Invincible," and other mines with well defined, and large ledges of high grade lead and silver ores were discovered in Coso Mining District, Inyo County, California, 130 miles by stage from "Allen's Camp," now Caliente, Kern County, Cal.

ORGANIZING OF THE COMPANY AND PROGRESS OF THE MINES.

Geo. W. Grayson, Archie Borland, S. B. Boswell, Clinton Gurnee, and Jesse S. Wall, organized a company called the Coso Consolidated Mining Company, and commenced work vigorously on the three first ledges with most satisfactory results. One shaft on the Bella Union was 100 feet deep on the 13th of July; shows three feet of galena and carbonate ores of high grade; average assays over $140 in silver and 60 per cent. lead.

One shaft on the Raleigh, forty feet deep shows a ledge over six feet wide; average assays, $106 per ton in silver and 50 per cent of lead. The character of these ores are such (containing sufficient iron and lime gang,) as to warrant the assertion that they will smelt as easily as the Cerro Gordo ores—which is well known to be the easiest smelting ores in the world.

This Company have over 5,000 feet of mining ground, cropping out boldly nearly the whole distance; the country rock is of soft whitish limestone, which is the most favorable in the country to warrant the ores going to a great depth. This kind of soft formation is not likely to cut off a vein of ore like the hard blue stratified lime stone.

This Company will continue to develop their mines until a large quantity of ore has accumulated on the dumps, sufficient to warrant the erection of two furnaces, when they will put them up and commence smelting.

This Company propose doing all this work, erecting furnaces, &c., without calling on the stockholders for assessments, having set aside 20,000 shares of their stock for a working capital for that purpose.

Office 402 Montgomery Street,
SAN FRANCISCO.

The Pacific Exchange.

When the first edition of the Stock Buyer's Manual was issued, there were but two Boards where Mining Stocks were bought and sold as a regular business. This business has so increased within the past few years that it was impossible for the San Francisco Stock Exchange to transact the business to the satisfaction of those most interested. Hence a number of gentlemen resolved to institute a new Board, and on the 6th of May last, was organized the Pacific Exchange, to which the charter members subscribed $5,000 each. The number being forty, gave this association the sum of $200,000 to start on, and forty other members were elected at once who also paid $5,000 each, which gave $200,000 more. The first opening of this Exchange for the transaction of business was on June 8th, 1875, in the large hall on the ground floor of the Halleck building, northeast corner of Sansome and Halleck streets, for which is paid the sum of $1,000 per month, rental. This is a very good hall one hundred feet long by fifty wide, and is fitted up in good style. Fifty feet at the front end of this building is fitted up for offices and Secretary's private room. On the opening of the Exchange a list of the leading mining stocks were put on the Board and called without charge.

A charge is made now however, of $500 to each mine, to have its stock placed on the list. On June 12th, the Exchange bought of Wm. Walkerley for $325,000, cash, an extensive property fronting forty feet on Montgomery street, next south of the Safe Deposit block,, and 137½ feet on the proposed extension of Leidesdorff street, and 46 9-12 on Pine. The depth of the lot from Montgomery to Leidesdorff street is 206 feet. It is designed by the Association to erect on this land, splendid buildings, including a hall for the sessions of the Exchange, which will be of ample dimensions.

The roll is called each day at 10:15 A. M., and 2:30 P. M. Regular call of stocks 11 A. M., and 3 P. M.

The business of buying and selling stocks has increased at a tremendous rate within a few years, and there are firms in this city such as Glazier & Co., that did in the months of December and January, 1874-5, five times as much business as did the entire San Francisco Stock Exchange in 1863-4, for the same months. The members of the Pacific Exchange are all men of wealth and strict business integrity, and their Association is destined to take high rank among similiar institutions in America.

We append a list of the officers and members:

E J. BALDWIN..President.
GEORGE S. DODGE..Vice-President.
GEO. C. HICKOX...Treasurer.
ANDREW J. MOULDER....................................Secretary.
JOSEPH TILDEN..Chairman.

Executive Committee.
ANSON GOLDSMITH.   DAVID HENRIQUES.

Finance Committee.
E. J. BALDWIN, *ex-officio*.   GEO. S. DODGE.
JAS. MCDONALD.   GEO. W. GRAYSON.

Committee on Membership.
WM. LENT.   A. W. WHITNEY.   M. BALDRIDGE.

Stock List Committee.
ROBERT SHERWOOD.   GEO. S. DODGE.   T. J. L. SMILEY.

Trust Fund Committee.
WM. LENT.   H. J. BOOTH.   JAMES MCDONALD.

LIST OF MEMBERS
—OF—
Pacific Stock Exchange.

Baldwin, E. J................513 California Street.
Baldridge, Michael...........Adjoining Pacific Exchange.
Barton, Robert...............422 Montgomery Street.
Bateman, I. C................419 California Street.
Beardsley, Paul F............Virginia City, Nevada.
Berry, Fulton G..............418 Montgomery Street.
Booth, H. J..................Hubbard & Johnson, NE cor San & Cal.
Boyd, John F.................419 California Street, Room 17.
Cavallier, Jules P...........513 California Street.

Clark, J. F.	405½ California St.
Cox, Jennings S.	Corner Commercial and Leidesdorff St.
Dodge, Geo. S	419 California Street.
Duncan, Wm. T.	405 California Street.
De Greayer, S.	308 Sansome Street.
Epstein, E	405½ California Street.
Fairbank, C. E.	309 California Street, Room 10.
Fay, Phillip S.	420 Montgomery Street.
Finlayson, J. R.	Corner Sansome and Halleck Streets.
Flugge, Carl	415 Montgomery Street.
Frank, Gustave	413 California Street.
Franks, Fred	331 Montgomery Street, Room 7.
Goldsmith, Anson	320 Sansome Street.
Gauthier, Eugene	424 Montgomery Street.
Grayson, G. W.	509 California Street.
Holmes, Ahira	N E cor. Clay and Mont. Streets.
Hearst, George	437 Pine Street.
Henriques, David	6 Leidesdorff Street.
Hickox, Geo. C	N E cor Mont. and Sacramento Sts.
Hickox, A. A.	Corner Sansome and Halleck Streets.
Hitchens, Jas	504 Montgomery Street.
Hoitt, Ira G	421 Montgomery Street.
Hosmer, D. M. (Bourne)	113 Leidesdorff Street.
Hunt, J. L.	306 Sansome Street.
Hutchinson, J	310 Montgomery Street.
Kyle, R. B.	5 Leidesdorff.
Lent, Wm. M. (McAneny)	419 California Street, Room 17.
Lincoln, Jonas	329 Montgomery Street.
Marks, Jos	419 California Street.
Martin, Minor S	426 Montgomery Street.
Mauldin, Hugh	Pacific Stock Exchange.
Minear, A. P. (Kent)	413 California Street.
Montealegre, Juan G.	329 Montgomery Street.
Moulder, Andrew J	Pacific Stock Exchange.
Moroney, Paul	Corner Sansome and Halleck Streets.
Marshall, Seth Jr.(Robinson)	311 California Street.
McCoppin, Frank	Pacific Stock Exchange.
McDonald, James M	N. W. cor Pine and Sansome Streets.
McCloud, E. A	405½ California Street.
Myers, Wm. F.	418 California Street.
Nash, J	405½ California Street.
Pinney, Geo. M.	402 Montgomery Street, Room 1
Phillip, Henry	205 Sansome Street.
Plummer, H. W	432 Montgomery Street.
Palmer, E. F.	413 California Street.
Riotte, E. N.	330 Pine Street.
Sanborn, T. C	Pacific Stock Exchange.
Scofield, D. G	113 Front Street.
Sherwood, Robert (Harvey)	108 Leidesdorff Street.
Smiley, T. J. L	310 Montgomery Street.
Smith, E. L	302 Montgomery Street, Rooms 1 & 2.
Stevens, C. (McGregor)	513 California Street.
Sutro, Gustave	415 Montgomery Street.

Swift, Frank................419 Cal. Street, Hayward's Building.
Taylor, Arthur C...........411½ California Street, Room 2.
Taylor, W. S................420 Montgomery Street.
Tilden, Jos................Pacific Stock Exchange.
Townsend, M. D...........106 Leidesdorff Street.
Todd, John M..............5 Leidesdorff Street.
Tyng, George...............309 California Street.
Vernon, Geo. R. (Tobin).....309 California Street, Room 10.
Webb, A. H.................402 Montgomery Street.
Weller, Chas. L.............419 Cal. St., Hayward's Bld'g, room 28.
Willard, G. H...............309 California Street.
Whitney, A. W.............Corner Sansome and Halleck Streets.
Whitney, J. G..............322 Turk Street.
Whiteley, Thomas..........205 Sansome Street.
Wood, H. P................331 Montgomery Street.
Wolf, F....................422 Montgomery Street.
Wright, Wm. H............420 Montgomery Street.
Yeazell, A. H..............113 Leidesdorff Street.

LOCAL DIRECTORY.

Trains on the C. P. R. R. leave San Francisco for the East at 8 o'clock A. M. daily; foot of Market street.

A through sleeping car runs to Virginia City on the regular train Sundays and Tuesdays; leave Virginia City, Mondays and Wednesdays; leave Sacramento, Sunday, Tuesday, Wednesday and Friday.

Oakland Ferries leave foot of Market street every half hour.

San Jose trains leave at 8:30 A. M. and 3:20 P. M. daily. Overland trains arrive at San Francisco at 5 o'clock P. M. daily; depot, Townsend and Fourth streets.

THEATRES.

California Theatre, between Kearny and Dupont, on Bush; performances commence at 8 o'clock P. M.

Maguire's New Theatre, Bush street, between Montgomery and Kearny.

Maguire's Opera House, opposite.

These are first-class places of amusement.

Stock Boards meet twice a day, viz.: at 11 A. M. and 3 P. M.

Banks open at 10 A. M.; close at 3 P. M., except Saturdays, when the hour for closing is 12 M.

STREET CARS.

Fare on all city railroads, 5 cents; except Lone Mountain and Sutter street lines: on these, four rides for 25 cents.

HOTELS.

Palace Hotel, price per day.		$4 00
Grand " "		4 00
Occidental "		3 00
Lick House "	$3 00 to	4 00
Russ House "	2 50 "	3 00
Cosmopolitan	2 50 "	3 00
Brooklyn	1 50 "	3 00
American Exchange	1 50 "	3 00
International "	1 50 "	3 00
Morton House	2 00 "	3 00

There are other hotels varying in price from $1 to $2.50 per day.

Lodging houses from 25 cents to $1 per night, each room.

Restaurant meals from 15 cents to $2.

WM. E. WOOD,
Commission Stock Broker,

331 Montgomery St. and 511 California St.

Office, Rooms 6 and 7.

M. BALDRIDGE,
Stock Broker,

OFFICE: HALLECK STREET, adjoining Pacific Stock Exchange, S. F.

Refers to JUDAH BAKER, WM. SHERMAN, U. S. Treasurer, D. J. STAPLES, President Fireman's Fund Insurance Company.

LOUIS C. HAGGIN,
Commission Stock Broker
(Member S. F. Stock Board,)

No. 439 CALIFORNIA STREET, San Francisco.

EDWIN F. CHILD, *Member S. F Stock Exchange.*   GEORGE E. MAGUIRE.

CHILD & MAGUIRE,
COMMISSION STOCK BROKERS,
TEMPORARILY AT

433 CALIFORNIA ST., SAN FRANCISCO.

H. W. PLUMMER & CO.,
Commission Stock Brokers,
(Member Pacific Board.)

309 Montgomery Street,   Room 1, Nevada Block,
San Francisco.

ARTHUR C. TAYLOR,
Member of Pacific Stock Exchange,

COMMISSION STOCK BROKER,
411½ California Street, Room 2.

Corrected List of Officers and Members of the Pacific Stock Exchange.

E. J. BALDWIN..President.
GEO. S. DODGE.....................................Vice-President.
GEO. C. HICKOX....................................Treasurer.
ANDREW J. MOULDER............................Secretary.
JOS. TILDEN...Chairman.

Jos. Tilden is also a member of the Finance Committee, and C. L. Weller is one of the Trust Fund Committee, in place of Mr. Booth. The officers are the same as that found in another place, with these two exceptions.

Baldwin, E. J., 513 California street.
Baldridge, Mich'l, Pacific Stock Exchange Building.
Barton, Rob't, 17 Nevada Block.
Beardsley, Paul F., Virginia City, Nevada.
Berry, Fulton G., 418 Montgomery street.
Boyd, John F., 17 Nevada Block.
Cavallier, Jules P., 513 California street.
Clark, J. F., Safe Deposit Building.
Cox, Jennings S., Nevada Block.
Dodge, Geo. S., Nevada Block.
Duncan, Wm. T., 405 California street.
De Greayer, S., 306 Sansome street.
Epstein, E., 411½ California street, room 2.
Fairbank, C. E., 309 California street, room 10.
Fay, Philip S., 420 Montgomery street.
Finlayson, J. R., Pacific Stock Exchange Building.
Flugge, Carl, 108 Leidesdorff street.
Frank, Gustave, 405½ California street.
Franks, Fred., 331 Montgomery street, room 7.
Goldsmith, Anson, Pacific Stock Exchange Building.
Gauthier, Eugene, 424 Montgomery street.
Grayson, G. W., Room 12, Stevenson's Building.
Holmes, Ahira, N. E. cor. Clay and Montgomery streets.
Hearst, George, 437 Pine street.
Heath, R. W., 424 Montgomery street, up stairs.
Henriques, David, Pacific Stock Exchange Building.
Hickox, Geo. C., S. E. cor. Pine and Montgomery streets.
Hickox, A. A., 302 Sansome streets.
Hitchens, Jas., 302 Sansome street.
Hoitt, Ira G., 421 Montgomery street.
Hosmer, D. M. (Bourne), 116 Halleck street.

G. H. WILLARD.   W. G. HUGHES.

WILLARD & HUGHES,
STOCK BROKERS,
309 CALIFORNIA ST.,   **SAN FRANCISCO.**

E. EPSTEIN.   ADAM PARKER.
Member Pacific Exchange.

E. EPSTEIN & CO.,
STOCK BROKERS,
411 1-2 California Street.

J. G. MONTELEAGRE & BROS.,
Stock and Money Brokers.

Money loaned on Stocks.   Stocks Bought and Carried on Margins.

SAFE DEPOSIT BUILDING, Room 5.

PHILLIP S. FAY,
Stock and Money Broker,
420 Montgomery Street.
ROOM No. 6.

IRA G. HOITT,
Stock and Money Broker,
421 Montgomery Street, San Francisco.

Loans negotiated on Stock and Collateral Securities.
Stocks Bought and Sold on Commission.

MEMBERS PACIFIC STOCK EXCHANGE.

Hunt, J. L., 304 Sansome street.
Hutchinson, J., 310 Montgomery street.
Johnson, Geo. H., Pacific Stock Exchange.
Kyle, R. B., 5 Leidesdrff street.
Lent, Wm. M. (McAneny), 419 California street, room 17.
Lincoln, Jonas, Rooms 12 and 13, Stevenson's Building.
Marks, Jos., 419 California street.
Martin, Minor S., 307 California street.
Mauldin, Hugh, 313 California street.
Minear, A. P. (Kent), 413 California street.
Montealegre, Juan G., Safe Deposit Building, Room 5.
Moulder, Andrew J., Pacific Stock Exchange.
Moroney, Paul, Pacific Stock Exchange Building.
Marshall, Seth, Jr. (Robinson), 311 California street.
McCloud, E. A., 405½ California street.
McDonald, James M., N. W. cor. Pine and Sansome streets.
Myers, Wm. F., 418 California street.
Nash, J., 405½ California street.
Phillip, Henry, 205 Sansome street.
Plummer, H. W., Nevada Block.
Palmer, E. F., 413 California street.
Rich, D., 422 Montgomery street.
Riotte, E. N., 330 Pine street.
Sanborn, T. C., Pacific Stock Exchange Building.
Scofield, D. G., 315 California street.
Sherwood, Rob't (Harvey), 108 Leidesdorff street.
Smiley, T. J. L., 310 Montgomery street.
Smith, E. L., 302 Montgomery street, Rooms 1 and 2.
Sutro, Gustave, 415 Montgomery street.
Taylor, Arthur C., 411½ California street, Room 2.
Taylor, W. S., 420 Montgomery street.
Tilden, Jos., Pacific Stock Exchange.
Tobin, R. C., Safe Deposit Building.
Townsend, M. D. 106 Leidesdorff street.
Todd, J. M., 410½ California street.
Tyng, George, 309 California street.
Van Ness, T. C., Safe Deposit Building.
Vernon, Geo. R. (Tobin), Safe Deposit Building.
Wattles, J. B., Pacific Mail Steamship Company.
Webb, A. H., 113 Leidesdorff street.
Weller, Chas. L., 419 California st., Hayward's Building, Room 28.
Willard, G. H. (Hughes), 309 California Street.
Whitney, J. G., Pacific Stock Exchange Building.
Whiteley, Thos. 205 Sansome street.
Wood, H. P., 331 Montgomery street and 511 California street.
Wolf, F., 422 Montgomery street.
Wright, Wm. H., 420 Montgomery street.
Yeazell, A. H., 113 Leidesdorff street.

G. H. PAGE,   JOHN SCOTT WILSON.   WM. HALE,
Late of John Taylor & Co.   *Member S. F. Stock Board.*

HALE, PAGE & WILSON,
Commission Stock Brokers,
No. 429 CALIFORNIA STREET,

MERCHANTS' EXCHANGE BUILDING.   SAN FRANCISCO.

J. R. HERRICK.   J. H. CONDRON.

J. R. HERRICK & CO.,
Commission Stock Brokers

326 MONTGOMERY STREET. San Francisco.

CHAS. C. HARVEY,
PACIFIC STOCK EXCHANGE.
STOCK BROKER,

108 Leidesdorff Street,   San Francisco.

FRANK McCOPPIN.   T. C. VAN NESS.

McCOPPIN, VAN NESS & CO.,
Commission Stock Brokers,

326 MONTGOMERY STREET,
SAN FRANCISCO.

R. F. KENT & CO.,
(Members Pacific Stock Exchange,)
COMMISSION STOCK BROKERS,

No. 413 California Street,   San Francisco.

Twenty per cent. required on all Orders to Buy or Sell Stock.

J. L. HUNT.   W. D. COATES.

HUNT & COATES,
Commission Stock Brokers,

306 Sansome St., Opp. Bank of California,
San Francisco.

M. S. MARTIN,
COMMISSION STOCK BROKER.

STOCKS
Bought, Sold, or Carried on Margin on Commission only.
(Member Pacific Stock Exchange.)

307 CALIFORNIA STREET,   SAN FRANCISCO.

Bankers,

SOUTHEAST CORNER PINE AND MONTGOMERY STREETS.

DEALERS IN

EXCHANGE,

Securities, Currency and Bonds.

STOCK ORDERS EXECUTED UPON COMMISSION.

HENRY P. WOOD,

Stock Broker,

331 Montgomery Street, *and* 511 California Street,

SAN FRANCISCO, CAL.

Horace L. Hill.   Lawrence Kilgour.

HILL & KILGOUR,

Stock and Money Brokers,

(Members of the San Francisco Stock Exchange.)

Transact a Strictly Commission Business in every description of Stocks, Bonds & Local Securities. Advances made on Approved Collaterals.

403 CALIFORNIA STREET, San Francisco.

Sunrise Silver Mining Company.

The property of this Company is located in Panamint, Inyo county, Cal., and consists of two mines, viz: "Sunrise" and "Twilight"—both free milling ore, the average assay of which was $50 per ton for croppings, and at 25 feet in depth, is $100. Native silver is sprinkled quite plentifully through the ore, and some single pieces, solid and pure, have been found weighing one ounce.

EACH CLAIM IS 1500 FEET IN LENGTH AND 600 IN WIDTH, AND EACH SHOWS THE SAME RICH CHARACTER OF ORE FOR SEVERAL HUNDRED FEET IN LENGTH.

The Company have erected a first-class 10-stamp mill; have five stamps completed and running on ore from Sunrise, part of which was the poorest in the mine. Forty days work of those five stamps have produced $20,000, one-half of which is net profit. When the other five stamps are completed and running on ore which assays $100 per ton, this Company can produce net, daily, $1,000, or $30,000 monthly.

It is rare to find a mine that from the very croppings has produced such a result and that has such bodies of the same kind of ore in sight as far as developments have been made, and we are confident that the SUNRISE has a future destined to be unsurpassed in prosperity by anything outside of the Big Bonanza. Permanent shafts, and other necessary developments, are now being pushed vigorously forward, and it is the intention of this Company to make their property a self-sustaining, paying institution, owning its own mills, doing an honest, legitimate business, to any act of which its officers or stockholders can refer with real pride.

This is an incorporated Company; capital stock, $50,000—shares $100 each. Title perfect. Office—318 California street, San Francisco.

T. B. WINGARD, Secretary.

Sullivan Mine, Gold Hill, Nevada.

TO CAPITALISTS.

The Sullivan Silver Mining Company desire to draw public attention to this valuable mining property located on the Comstock Lode, situated at the east end of Gold Hill city, 2,500 feet east of Belcher, 2,400 north of Justice, 2,600 feet north of Woodville, 3,000 feet east of Overman, 4,000 feet south of Julia, and 8,500 feet south of Consolidated Virginia and California mines, in a direct line between the Justice and Julia mines, and on the same line with the Consolidated Virginia and California ore bodies.

The Company desire, from developments being made, to call the attention of mining men and capitalists to this part of the Comstock lode.

This mine was located July 17th, 1873, by John Sullivan of Gold Hill, and contains 1,300 lineal feet on the vein. The first shaft sunk was to the depth of 75 feet, and drifts were run from it following the ledge. A considerable amount of good milling ore, paying $25 to $30 to the ton was found. At that depth, the ledge, which is 30 feet wide between the walls, was of low grade and it was obvious that a further depth was only necessary to develop a paying mine, and to accomplish this is the object which the Company have now in view in offering for sale a portion of their shares. Upon the recommendation of three practical Comstock miners, who have thoroughly surveyed the whole property, the Company have located a new shaft 480 feet south of the old one, which gives better facilities for developing the mine. The necessary grading has been done preparatory to erecting the hoisting works, and a good road has also been built connecting the mine with the Virginia and Truckee railroad.

At a depth of 42 feet, in the new shaft, the east clay wall was struck, and in continuing the shaft down to 72 feet, 30 feet of ledge formation was disclosed, the ledge dipping at a slight angle to the east. At the same time the Company are running an adit level at the rate of 25 feet per week, to connect the adit level with the main shaft.

The ledge matter is entirely the same as the Consolidated Virginia. The shaft consists of three compartments: two of them 4x5, and the other 5x5 in the clear, and framed with 12-inch square timber.

By recent survey it is ascertained that at the surface the shaft of the Sullivan Mine is 300 feet lower than the surface of the shaft of the Consolidated

Virginia, and is unquestionably now in the same body of ore as that great mine.

The report of Dr. Linderman, Superintendent of the United States Mint, says he made a personal examination of the Consolidated Virginia and California, and that there was in sight millions of dollars worth of ore in each of these mines, and that the Comstock lode seemed inexhaustable—was better and richer than the famous Potosi mines of Mexico. Twelve months ago the stock of the above mines was selling at less than $40 per share; since then it has gone as high as $800 per share, making fortunes for those who invested and held their stock.

The Sullivan mine is producing ore so much like that of the Consolidated Virginia and California as to give assurance that it will be as valuable as these mines. There is a chance to make a fortune for a small outlay. It is certainly worth investigating. The news from the mine is full of hope and encouragement, and the work is progressing rapidly. The causes which led to the testing of this now valuable ground was its central location. The fact that the mine has something on which to predicate this statement is a truth that will not be denied by any person after visiting the mine and its location.

From the Gold Hill *News* (extract):

"This well known mining location, lying in the Comstock ravine, having passed into the proprietorship of men of capital and enterprise, is now being actively developed and brought into deserved prominence."

Superintendent's letter, October 3d, says:

"We opened a large vein of ledge formation in the Sullivan new shaft yesterday."

Superintendent's letter, October 16th, says.

"The shaft is now 60 feet in depth. We have 20 feet of ledge. We are working 18 men, and will increase our force as soon as we have room for them."

Superintendent's letter, October 19th, says:

"We have 25 feet ledge formation in the shaft, and still no west wall. Commenced drain tunnel Friday last; it will connect with main shaft at a depth of 150 feet from surface."

Superintendent's letter, October 23d, says:

"Struck west wall in drain tunnel Wednesday last. It is a heavy clay wall. We have the east wall in shaft, west wall in drain tunnel. Thickness from wall to wall, 162 feet. Ore deposits in this vast formation may be looked for at any time."

Superintendent's letter, October 30th, says:

"Shaft 72 feet deep; tunnel in 115 feet; both in the same Comstock formation. Taking samples of ore daily; some giving good assays."

Superintendent's letter, November 1st. says:

"The face of adit level to-day is clay, porphyry and quartz; same formation as that in shaft."

Superintendent's letter, November 6th, says:

"We have now 42 feet of ledge formation in tunnel Indications of an ore deposit is very flattering."

SULLIVAN MINE.

Superintendent's letter, November 9th, says:

"Pushing adit level at the rate of 25 feet per week. We are passing through as fine a ledge formation as there is on the Comstock. Length of tunnel to-day, 135 feet; 60 feet of ledge formation. Survey completed. Thickness of ledge matter, from wall to wall, 162 feet."

Extract from the Gold Hill *News* of November 11, 1875:

"SULLIVAN.—The tunnel is in 165 feet, and is being pushed ahead night and day, continuing in the same excellent Comstock matter heretofore mentioned. Less than 150 feet will bring the tunnel to a connection with the shaft, and from the assays obtained, a good ledge of pay ore should be found within that distance."

The balance of the working capital set aside by the Company for development, can be secured from any of the Directors, A. K. P. Harmon, S. E. Holcombe, L. Barris, E. J. Baldwin, Charles C. Smith, or at the office of the Company, Room 13, Safe Deposit Building, No. 326 Montgomery street, San Francisco.

O. H. BOGART, Secretary.

H. P. GREGORY & CO., 14 & 16 First St., S. F.

SOLE AGENTS FOR PACIFIC COAST FOR Blake's Patent STEAM PUMP.

Over 5,000 in use in the United States.

Every Pump fully guaranteed to do the Work recommended.

Bear in mind the fact that the improved BLAKE PUMP has no Piston Valve. The Steam Piston is now driven by means of two common Slide Valves. All parts liable to wear are compensating. Every Water Cylinder is *Brass Lined*. It is never necessary to remove the Pump from its position for repairs. All Pumps of corresponding sizes being exact duplicates any part which might accidentally become broken can be at once replaced.

H. H. SCOTT & CO., Stock Brokers, 307 Montgomery St.

MACHINERY

FOR MINES,

Such as Engines, Hoisting Rigs, Blowers, Pumps, Turbine Wheels, Machinists' Tools, Iron Pipe, Belting, etc.. etc. Send to

TREADWELL & CO., San Francisco.

Our Mining Engines

With Double Drums, Locomotive Boiler, Double Cylinders and Reverse motions, make the most complete hoisting works for shafts 500 or 1500 feet, that have yet been built. These Engines may be seen in the Ophir, Chollar, Belcher, Con. Virginia, Europa, Niagara, Leviathan, C. & C. Shaft, Phil. Sheridan, North Con. Virginia, and other well known mines on the Comstock. For sale only by

TREADWELL & CO., San Francisco.

W. I. TUSTIN'S PATENT
First Premium Windmills & Horse Powers.

The simplicity and perfection of these Machines is the result of twenty-six years' experience in California.

We have made the manufacture of Pumping Machinery a specialty for the past twenty-six years in California.

Received all the First Premiums awarded by the Mechanics' Institute for the past eigth years in our line.

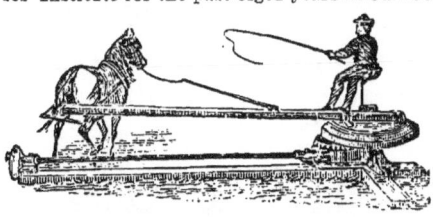

The "Economy" at work.

Economy.

These Powers are designed for all purposes, such as Pumping Water for Irrigation, Watering Stock, Chopping Feed, Churning, Sawing Wood, Running Machinery for Manufacturing, Mechanical, or other purposes.

Tanks, Pumps, Piping and every variety of Machinery and Goods connected with this line of business furnished to order, at the lowest market prices. Send for Descriptive Circular and Price List.

Factory, cor. Market and Beale Sts., San Francisco.

S. B. WAKEFIELD,
(S. F. Stock & Ex. Board,)
Stock and Exchange Broker,
313 CALIFORNIA ST., SAN FRANCISCO.

Commission business exclusively.

TYNG & BULLARD,
(Pacific Stock Exchange,)
STOCK BROKER,
Offices 8 & 9, 309 California Street, SAN FRANCISCO, CAL.

(Commission Business only.)

WILLIAM L. DUNCAN,
Stock Broker,
424 Montgomery Street, San Francisco, Cal.

Liberal advances made on active stocks.

COPE, UHLER & CO.
Commission Stock Brokers.
503 CALIFORNIA ST,, San Francisco.

HOSMER & BOURNE,
Stock Brokers,
Cor. Leidesdorff and Halleck Sts.. SAN FRANCISCO, CAL.

Post Office Address, Lock Box 1837.

B. F. SHERWOOD & CO.,
Stock and Money Brokers,
No. 406½ California Street, San Francisco.

STATE AND CITY SECURITIES, MINING STOCKS AND BONDS,
BOUGHT AND SOLD STRICTLY ON COMMISSION.

A. A. HICKOX,   H. G. KUHL.
HICKOX, KUHL & CO.
Stock Brokers,
N. E. cor. Sansome & Halleck Sts., San Francisco.

MEMBERS PACIFIC STOCK EXCHANGE.

Paul's Dry Amalgamating Process

A CHEAP SYSTEM FOR WORKING

GOLD AND SILVER ORES.

Its combined merits challenge the Metallurgical skill of the age to surpass
(SECURED BY SEVEN LETTERS PATENT.)

Having completed my labors for the perfecting of this system, I am now ready to contract for the furnishing of machinery for MILLS, of any capacity, from five to one hundred tons per day, and assert my ability to increase the yield of all Gold Mills, working by the wet battery, copper-plates and blankets, from **50 to 100 per cent.** In working silver ores by *raw* amalgamation from 20 to 200 per cent.—according to the combination of metals.

The mechanical arrangement is such that all feeding, crushing, pulverizing, transmission of ores, amalgamating and concentration is done mechanically, and every feature of it practically demonstrated by the working of HUNDREDS OF TONS OF ORE, with results exceeding any before obtained, by from 50 to 100 per cent. Mills are practically at work in the mountains, which can be visited.

Parties engaged in Quartz Mining, and intending to erect Mills, will find it to their advantage to adopt my machinery and system, and I invite such to an investigation and examination of plans and machinery for same. Pamphlets forwarded on receipt of address.

PAUL'S PATENT
PULVERIZING BARREL,
FOR THE REDUCTION OF
Quartz to an Impalpable Powder.
DRY.

The attention of the mining public is now called especially to this Pulverizer, which I have brought to a complete state of perfection, as one of the most thorough, durable and cheap modes of bringing ore to an impalpable powder.

They can be made of any size, and to perform any amount of work required from five tons to one hundred per day, receiving ore, coarsely reduced.

These Barrels are made SELF-FEEDING and SELF-DISCHARGING. All ore is reduced to any desired fineness, without inconvenience from dust.

1st. The reducing material is coarser-quartz pulverizing, by attrition, the finer. As the Barrel revolves, all ore sufficiently reduced passes out of the way, leaving that unreduced to have all the advantages of attrition.

2d. Not having to pay for iron as a reducing agent, using the quartz from your mine instead, you turn what heretofore has been an expense to a very considerable profit. In fact, this feature alone will more than pay the wear and tear bills of the whole machinery connected with the Paul Process.

3d. In consequence of using no iron as a reducing agent, your ore prepared for amalgamation is freed of granulated iron, which is one of the greatest annoyances in amalgamation, a cause of much of the loss of precious metals in milling ores. All experienced amalgamators understand this.

The wear and tear is trifling. By the speed given to the barrel, which is in accordance to diameter, the wear is taken almost entirely off of the periphery plates, and thrown upon and into the material itself, thus saving iron, and putting the wear as desired. These Barrels will last for years; all that in time may need repairing are the inside linings, which are inexpensive and easily replaced. These Barrels are no experiment; on the contrary, they have been severely and practically tested.

Parties interested can gain all further particulars by applying to

ALMARIN B. PAUL,
318 California Street, (up stairs,) San Francisco.

TABLE OF CONTENTS
AND INDEX.

	PAGE.
Pacific Coast Mines and their Productions	3
Trojan Mining Company	5
Atlantic Consolidated Gold and Silver Mine	6
South End, Faught, and DeForest Mines	8
Tahoe, Leviathan, and Cromer Mines	9
Eldorado Silver Mining Co	10
Lee Gold and Silver Mining Co	11
Mining Districts of Nevada and California	12
How to Deal in Mining Stock	14
Morning Star Mining Co	15
Edinburgh Mining Co	16
Hints and Suggestions to Stock Dealers	17
Highest and Lowest of Stock, 1875	18
Silver Sprout Mining Co	19
Virginia Consolidated Mine	20
Electric Mining Co	21
New Coso Mining Co	22
Coso Consolidated Co	23
Pacific Exchange	24
Sunrise Silver Mining Co	38
Sullivan Silver Mining Co	39

STOCK BUYER'S MANUAL.

Introductory	3
S. F. Stock Exchange	5
California Stock Exchange	12
Tabular Statements of Mines	14
Panamint Mining District	27
Cerro Gordo Mining District	36
Calistoga Mine	42

NATIONAL PROSPECTING AND MINING COMPANY.

Principal Office, Merchants' Exchange Building, California Street, San Francisco; Eastern Office, No. —— Chestnut Street, Phila.

This company is an organization for the purpose of buying, selling and locating mining lands and claims. It also organizes mining companies, places the stock, and attends to the erection of mills and furnaces upon mines already discovered. The company extends its operations throughout the entire mining regions of the Pacific Coast, and will have branch offices in all the principal cities of the United States and Europe. Specimens of ores of the precious metals can be seen at their offices, and full information obtained in regard to the mineral products of the most valuable mining districts in the United States. This company is organized under the most flattering auspices, the officers being well-known gentlemen of ability, and those at all interested in mines or minerals should not fail to give them a call.

WM. H. WILCOX, President.   JOHN W. MORRIS, Vice-Prest.
T. LATHAM WISWALL, Sec'y.   H. H. HOBBS, Treasurer.

Directors.

WM. H. WILLCOX,   JOHN W. MORRIS,
T. LATHAM WISWALL,   HIRAM H. HOBBS,
WALTER J. WELCH,   GEORGE T. TRUMAN.
WM. R. ARMSTRONG.

LAFAYETTE E. SEAMAN, General Manager.

CHARLES E. CONVIS, Stock and Money Broker, No. 9 Halleck's Building. Take Elevator to Third Floor.

Entered according to Act of Congress, in the year 1875, by

H. M. VAN ARNAM,

in the Office of the Librarian of Congress, at Washington.

INTRODUCTORY.

In this little book is herewith given what its name designates: —The Stock Buyers' Manual and Hand-Book of Reference. By it can be seen at a glance the entire status of every mine whose stock is sold in this city. By reference to the map, its location may be seen, and we have added a description of the famous Panamint Mine, which is justly named the wonder of the world. We make no pretensions to authorship as a work of literary merit, but as giving exact information to the public in regard to the most important among our Pacific Coast interests. To all the city papers we are indebted for much information, and thank the *Post*, *Chronicle* and *Alta* for the interesting matter contained in their columns. The *Bulletin* and *Call*, while being conservative in regard to mining excitements, always can be relied on to give facts concerning the best interests of our people in mines, and are willing to incur any expense in order that they may give the news.

Our tables and much valuable information has been kindly furnished by the proprietors of the *Daily Stock Report*, to whom we desire to make our acknowledgment. This paper is invaluable to those interested in mines and mining stocks, and no one who engages in this business should be without it. The publication office is on Sacramento street near Montgomery, and we would commend it to the public.

The dealing in stocks has become as much of a legitimate business in this city and at Virginia City (Nevada), as is any other business. It is something to which men of intelligence and shrewdness give their time and attention and risk their money. It has been called a gambling operation, but this is what makes the business attractive, for in the breast of every individual man, and woman, in the land there is a desire to take risk. It is also true "that there seems to be very little mining stock changing hands of those mines that are paying a regular dividend, because those mines are sure. When the "Bonanza" is struck the stock rises to its limit and then remains at a fixed price, the holders will not sell, expecting their regular dividends, and hold it as an investment. It is the mines that are located in the same ranges with big strikes that have already been made that afford the speculator the opportunity of risking money on the chances of making a strike. Those times are the ones that offered opportunities for those who feel inclined to risk their coin. There are, perhaps, 50,000 people in San Francisco who are directly or indirectly interested in stocks. The sounds and clamors of the Stock Exchange not only reach the crowd which is always to be found on California street, but reverberates among the hills and mountains throughout the State, and can be even heard at the foot of Mount Davidson, and the report of sales is eagerly looked for even in Utah and New York.

The mines of California, of Nevada, of Arizona and of Oregon are in their infancy. The mountains are full of precious metals of all descriptions; the great strikes are yet to be made, and it may be that the mine the stock of which is the lowest price in the Board at present will show the most ore in a few months. Hence it is folly to attempt to be sure of making a selection in buying stocks. Like any other venture, it is attended with risks, and luck may attend any one. Our stock dealers are fair and honorable as a class, and any of them will treat their customer with all proper courtesy and respect.

HISTORY
OF THE
San Francisco Stock and Exchange Board.

The following sketch of this institution was obtained from Franklin Lawton, Secretary of the Board, who has been connected with it since its organization. In the Spring of 1861, the mining excitement commenced in real earnest. At that time the owners of mines, and those parties who were directly interested in them, were in the habit of making contracts and sales themselves of portions of their interests, and sales of "feet" were made to each other whenever or wherever they chanced to meet. This practice soon called into existence a new set of brokers, as those who had previously engaged in this business dealt chiefly in Water Stock, Gas Stock, Bonds, Notes, Securities, etc. The mines of the celebrated Comstock lode were at this time entirely in feet, very few of them having been divided into shares, as is now the universal custom. The manner of selling feet was productive of so much fraud and chicanery, and gave the mine owners such an advantage that it became almost hopeless for an outsider to attempt to get a fair chance for his investment. An illustration will be given to explain this more fully. Some of the large mine owners would meet and make a pretended sale, one to the other; then an agent, or some one of their own number, would go down to the "Bank Exchange," where the brokers usually congregated, and report that a certain number of feet had been sold in such or such a mine for so many dollars per foot. This would give an impetus to this mine and establish the price for that day. After having "been bit" several times in this manner it became old, and those interested desired something else. This was one of the main incentives to induce several of the brokers to found and establish a Board similar to the Exchange Board of New York. Franklin Lawton, Esq., suggested to several of those brokers that they meet together and establish or organize a regular Exchange Board. His suggestion met with much favor from some and was vehemently opposed by others. Those who favored the scheme met together to the number of five. The matter was discussed at some length and met with much opposition from the large mine owners and dealers, who imagined that it would open the door for a lot of adventurous speculators, who could have an even chance to earn a few dollars by their abilities as financiers in dividing profits of sales on mines. These malcontents were subsequently glad to become members of the Board and pay a high fee for so doing.

Finally, by great persuasion, a dozen of the most prominent brokers were induced to sign articles of association for the purpose of forming a Stock Exchange on the mode of the New York Stock Exchange, with the direct view of facilitating the buying and selling of stocks and for the protection of the members. The articles were as follows:

SAN FRANCISCO, Sept. 1, 1862.

For the purpose of facilitating the purchase and sale of stock and mutual security, we the undersigned propose to organize a San Francisco Stock Exchange, on the plan of the New York Stock and Exchange Board. In furtherance of which object we do each agree to pay into the hands of the Treasurer, when chosen, the sum of $100 :

J. PERRY, JR.
T. C. SANBORN.
S. HEYDENFELDT.
GEO. R. BARCLAY.
H. C. LOGAN.
ROBERT C. PAGE.
C. H. WAKELEE.
JOSEPH GRANT.
J. B. E. CAVALLIER.
S. C. BRUCE.
P. C. HYMAN.
HENRY CRITCHER.
P. B. CORNWALL.
N. A. WATSON.
WM. L. HIGGINS.
E. J. DE STA MARINA.
SIMON MAYER.
FRANKLIN LAWTON.
D. C. WILLIAMS.

HENRY SCHMEIDELL.
H. P. WAKELEE.
E. W. TEACLE.
O. ABBOTT.
R. E. BREWSTER.
A. MARRIUS CHAPELLE.
E. DUPRE.
A. J. SHIPLEY.
R. H. SINTON.
T. A. TALBERT.
WM. WILLSON LAWTON.
FRANK M. PIXLEY.
DAVID HENRIQUES.
WM. H. PARKER.
WM. R. GARRISON.
J. DOWNE WILSON.
A. VAN LOKEREN.
CHAS. K. SMITH.

The first meeting, called for the purpose of organizing the Stock Board was held on the 8th day of September, 1862, at the office of J. B. E. Cavallier, R. C. Page, Joseph Grant, and Samuel Bruce, who were then engaged in the real estate and general brokerage business. Their office was at 428 Montgomery street.

These gentlemen, together with Messrs. Franklin Lawton, Theodore C. Sanborn, E. J. Santa Marina, Henry Schmeidell, John Perry, Jr., and T. W. Teacle, were most active in their efforts to found the institution.

At this meeting temporary officers were elected, viz: Mr. Henry Schmeideli as Chairman *pro tem.*, and Mr. Frank Lawton as Secretary *pro tem.* A Committee of six was also chosen to draft a Constitution and By-Laws for the Board, namely: Messrs. Perry, Sanborn, Critcher, Page, Henriques and Lawton.

Messrs. Shipley, Chapelle, Wakelee, Grant and Watson were appointed a Committee of Arrangements.

At the next meeting, held Sept. 11, 1862, the Constitution was reported by the Committee and adopted by the meeting, and permanent officers of the "San Francisco Stock and Exchange Board" were balloted for and elected as follows:

J. B. E. CAVALLIER..................................President
E. W. TEACLE...................................Vice-President
FRANKLIN LAWTON....................................Secretary
HENRY SCHMEIDELL...................................Treasurer

At a meeting held Sept. 12, 1862, By-Laws were reported by the Committee, and after some modification were adopted.

The original fee or assessment on the organization of the Board was $100 for membership; but it was only found necessary to assess $50 to each member to make up a fund of $2,000. A small room was then rented in Montgomery Block for the use of the Board. It was furnished with a plain table in horse-shoe form, desks for the Preident, Secretary, etc.

At first business in the Board was very dull, the members, with two or three exceptions, being very inexperienced in stock transactions on the Exchange Board.

Shortly after the Board was fully organized business began to increase, and many new applications for membership were received. The Board thereupon concluded to increase their numbers. At first the initiation fee had been fixed at one hundred dollars, and a few members were admitted at that sum. The fee was then increased to two hundred and fifty dollars, then to five hundred, and finally to one thousand dollars. And the number of members was limited to eighty, which limit has been maintained to the present day. The funds of the Board soon accumulated to $25,000; and from that day to this they have never lacked for money for their own uses, and for many very large and praiseworthy charities. Concerning some of their donations we will speak hereafter.

After occupying this room in Montgomery Block a while the Board found it entirely too small for their purposes, and they removed to the building opposite, at the S. W. corner of Washington and Montgomery streets, belonging to Mr. Michael Reese.

The Board remained here for some six or eight months, and then found this also inadequate to their wants, and again moved, this time to a large room in the building over the old Metropolitan Theater, the west side of Montgomery street between Washington and Jackson streets, built expressly for the members of the Board by Mr. Eugene Sullivan. That is the same room where the Fifteenth District Court is now held. This room was built under the supervision of Messrs. Cavallier and Lawton, then President and Secretary of the Board, and was the most convenient and comfortable room ever occupied by the Board.

About the time of this last removal, the Bank of California was moved to the new building on California street, where it now is, and other moneyed institutions congregating on California street, or in its neighborhood, which began to be the moneyed centre of the city.

When the New Merchants' Exchange Building on California street between Montgomery and Sansome was erected, it was with the understanding that the Board should occupy a room in it, and the Board took stock in this building to the amount of $20,000, which they still own. They moved from the Metropolitan Theater to the Merchants' Exchange, and occupied the room designed for them, on completion of the building, when, finding it inconvenient and not large enough, they removed for the last time to the room they occupy at present in Duncan's Building, 411½ California street, (south side of California street between Montgomery and Sansom.

Since the establishment of the Board there has been several excitements in stocks, among which may be mentioned the strike in the Gould & Curry Mine, when the shares ran up in a few days to $6,000 each; then Justice was "way up"; then Savage went to $700; then Crown Point and Belcher, and more recently the Bonanza strike in Consolidated Virginia sent this stock up to $800 in about 60 days. All other stocks sympathized with these and stocks were very active. Fortunes were made in a day, and people who one day were in ordinary circumstances in life, the next day would start on a trip to Europe. It is proper, however, to remark that among those who are suddenly made rich in this city by a sudden appreciation in the value of stocks, seldom betray the parvenue or can be classed among "shoddyites."

THE CHARITIES OF THE SAN FRANCISCO STOCK AND EXCHANGE BOARD

Have been most remarkable. Large sums have been voted to aid the Orphan Asylum at various times; when Chicago had its baptism of fire a wail of distress resounded throughout the land. This institution responded promptly and effectively.

During the past Winter (1874-5), Marysville was inundated, and this Board immediately sent to their relief $10,000. General Brisbin, of the U. S. A., came from Omaha and went before the Board, and in simple, eloquent and pathetic language, told the members, of the suffering and distress of the people of Nebraska on account of grasshoppers. In less than twenty minutes the Board had voted as a body $1,000, and the individual members gave over $8,000 more. These things show that, however anxious and eager these gentlemen are to make money, their hearts are tender and pockets open ever at the call of suffering humanity.

LIST OF STOCKS CALLED.

A list of local and mining stocks was made up by the Board at that time without any charge.

The following is taken from the Records of the Board, and exhibits the first five days' business done after organization, commencing

Friday, September 26, 1862.

SELLER.	BUYER.	QUANTITY.	STOCK.	PRICE.	TIME.	REMARKS.
Perry	Logan	$500	Starr	$387½	....	....
Marina	Sanborn	10 feet	Chollar	185	....	....
Perry	Pixley	50 shares	Mt. Davidson	8	....	....

FRANKLIN LAWTON, Secretary.

Saturday, Sept. 27, 1862.

Perry	Logan	5 shares	Cal. Navigation	39½	....	....

FRANKLIN LAWTON, Secretary.

Monday, Sept. 29, 1862.

SELLER.	BUYER.	QUANTITY.	STOCK.	PRICE.	TIME.	REMARKS.
Perry	Logan	3000	S. F. Bonds	70½	....	....
Wilson	Perry	6 feet	Esmeralda	50	....	....

FRANKLIN LAWTON, Secretary.

Tuesday, Sept. 30, 1862.

Logan	Cavallier	50 feet	Desert	12½	....	....
Sanborn	Cavallier	10 feet	Potosi	187	....	....

FRANKLIN LAWTON, Secretary.

Wednesday, Oct. 1, 1862.

Marina	Cavallier	15 feet	Chollar	175	....	....
E.H.Wakelee	Mayer	10 feet	Sierra Nevada	140	....	....
Perry	Shipley	20 shares	Mt. Davidson	6½	....	....
Logan	Perry	10 feet	Meredith	20	....	....
Logan	Hyman	36½ feet	"	20	....	....
Perry	Sanborn	7 shares	BensleyWaterCo	35	....	....

FRANKLIN LAWTON, Secretary.

In addition to this we exhibit an hour's sales of ten of the leading stocks sold Friday, April 9th, 1875:

SHARES.	NAMES.	AMOUNT.	SHARES.	NAMES.	AMOUNT.
320	Belcher..................	$37½	589	Ophir.....................	$100
515	Best & Belcher..........	52½	480	Overman................	63
780	Crown Point.	39½	300	Raymond & Ely..........	49¼
1190	California.................	63	470	Imperial.................	8½
1205	Lady Bryan..............	6	600	Meadow Valley..........	7½

This, too, is not during a mining stock excitement, but the pulse is calm and even. Thus can be seen how much the business has grown in a few years.

OFFICERS AND MEMBERS

OF THE

S. F. STOCK BOARD.

President,
JAS. R. KEENE.

Vice-President,
COLL DEANE.

Chairman,
B. H. COIT.

Treasurer,
H. SCHMEIDELL.

Secretary,
F. LAWTON.

Brooks, S H
Bonynge, C W
Boswell, S B
Brown, J W
Budd, W C
Burling, Wm
Burtsell, J M
Cahill, E
Cantin, J P
Charles, H A
Child, E F
Coit, B H
Coleman, J W
Coursen, G A
Crocker, J H
Cope, G W
Deane, Coll

Dixon, S
Duncan, W L
Everett, A F
Eyre, E E
Ford, J C
Fitch, J R
Foster, W H
Freeborn, J
Fox, C W
Glover, G F M
Glazier, I
Greenebaum, J
Hall, E F
Hill, H L
Herr, J J
Hopkins, C H
Hubbard, C V D
Higgins, W L
Hassey, F A
Henriques, David
Ives, G I
Jones, G H
Keene, J R
Kenney, Chas A
King, Jos L
Kilgour, L
Kinsey, A G
Knox, G T
Latham, J H
Lissak, A H
Logan, H C
Loveland, L F

Lawton, Franklin
Lynch, J
Mahony, J H, Jr
Marina, E J de S
McDonald, M L
McDonald, M J
McKenty, J
Noble, H H
Parker, W C
Page, R C
Peckham, E P
Perry, J
Rogers, R F
Rorke, B B
Schmeidell, H
Shawhan, J E
Shotwell, J M
Smiley, G W
Stanford, W T
Stoutenborough, C
Steinhart, S
Sherwood, B F
Thornburgh, W B
Turnbull, Walter
Vimont, J N
Williams, H
Whitney, A W
Wilke, F E
Woods, F H
Winans, J C
Zinns, L A

The California Stock Exchange.

The business of dealing in stocks is not confined entirely to the San Francisco Stock and Exchange Board. The number of members of that institution being limited to 80, and it being inconvenient to have a larger number, it was resolved by several gentlemen to start a new Board for the purpose of dealing in stocks. Consequently, on the first of January, 1872, the organization of the California Stock Exchange was effected by John Middleton (since deceased), J. Y. L. Smiley, Jack McKenty, S. Burrel, S. Hunneman, W. W. Lawton, Geo. W. Ramage, M. D. Townsend, Wm. H. Wright, Henry S. Fitch, Chas. L. Weller, E. L. Smith, A. C. Chick, J. K. Kloppenstein, G. De Sta. Marina, Henry C. Logan, M. Rudsdale, J. P. Cantin, Wm. H. Brown, Wm. Jay Smith, T. J. Poulterer, T. S. Sanborn, George Rogers, J. H. Owens, S. Marks, E. J. White, C. A. Keeny, Geo. S. Sorin, John Harper, T. B. Pheby, J. F. Crossett, A. Diftot, R. F. Kent, F. Walf, Chas. Hosmer, E. S. Tibbey, R. Broderick, E. J. Baldwin. C. C. Harney, W. D. Williams (since deceased). The first officers elected were as follows: President, Thos. J. Poulterer; Vice-President, T. J. L. Smiley; Secretary, Wm. W. Lawton; Treasurer, E. J. Baldwin; Caller, Joseph Tilden. At the commencement this body had not so much difficulty in making up a list of stocks as the old Board, as the list was already made, and the members had only to secure business. This was not difficult, and soon the business began to increase. The limit to the number of members was at first 70, but it has been reduced, so that the present limit is 62. The business is now quite large, and is increasing daily. The daily city papers all give each day the amount of stock sold, and it only needs a glance at their columns to give the intelligent reader an idea of the magnitude of this business.

The manner of doing business and of conducting sales and purchases, is precisely the same in both Boards; and as we have omitted giving it in our sketch of the San Francisco Stock Exchange, we will describe it here. When the hour of commencing has arrived, the Caller (he who calls the list) mounts the rostrum, and calls the stock in alphabetical order; then those who desire to sell and buy leave their seats, and rushing into the center of the room, announce that they will give so much for so many shares, or will sell so many shares at such a price. Although to an inexperienced spectator all is confusion and unintelligible, the Caller understands every word, and the clerks and reporters sitting at the desk jot down sales as fast as they are made. In a few minutes the Caller brings down the gavel sharply and has the sales called off, when if there are any corrections made it must be done at once, or it not the sale is confirmed. Thus an hour is passed, and an incredible amount of business has been done—sometimes to the amount of a million dollars in one hour. The scene is very exciting, and although all seems to be clamor and noise, it is nevertheless great monetary transactions. The time for holding the California Stock Exchange is one hour in the morning of each day, commencing at 10:15, and in the afternoon commencing at 2:15, ending at 3:15. The funds on hand now are ample, and the Board is flourishing. Business is increasing, and instead of detracting from the business of the old Board, the competition seems to be adding to it.

The location of this Board-room is at the end of Leidesdorff street, near the office of the National Gold Bank and Trust Company, which institution is the present Treasurer of this Board. Attached will be found a full list of the officers and members:

OFFICERS AND MEMBERS

OF THE

CALIFORNIA STOCK EXCHANGE.

President,
T. J. L. SMILEY.

Vice-President,
C. L. WELLER.

Secretary,
W. W. LAWTON.

Caller,
JOS. TILDEN.

Treasurer,
NATIONAL GOLD
BANK & TRUST
COMPANY.

Armstrong, J L
Baldridge, M
Barrell, Sam'l
Beales, John T
Bourne, J B
Bradford, T D
Brumagim, J W
Conger, C C

Den, N C V
DeGreaver, S
Dore, Benjamin
Duncan, W T
Finlayson, J R
Flagg, H H
Franks, Fred'k
Gautier, E
Gunter, A C
Hart, Thos R
Hendrie, E B
Harvey, C C
Hawkins, Jas J E
Hoare, C W
Hoitt, I G
Holmes, A
Hosmer & Bourne
Hikox, A A
Hunt, J L
Hutchinson, J
Hyneman, S
Johnson, Geo H
Kent, R F
Klopenstine, J
Kreider, F H
Lawton, W W
Lincoln, J

Luty, Fred E
Marina, J de S
McDonnell, J H
McHaffie, J H
Morhardt, P F
Parker, J D
Plummer, H W
Reynolds, W T
Rich, D
Robbins, E V
Roberts, D S
Schmitt, C A
Schmitt, M
Smith, E L
Smith, W Jay
Smiley, T J L
Soren, Geo S
Sweet, H A
Sutherland, S F
Taylor, W S
Thompson, W M
Tilden, Jos
Todd, J M
Weller, Chas L
Wolf, F
Wright, Wm H
Yeagell, A H

We do not give amount of bullion produced, but nearly all these mines are producing and work on them is progressing.

CALIFORNIA MINES.

Companies.	No. Am't in Mine	No. Ft. in Mine	No. Shares in Mine.	Last Assessment Levied.	Am't per Sh.	Am't per Ft.	No. D'v'ds	Last Dividend.	Total Am't Ass's Levied	Total Am't Div'ds Dis'd	Remarks.
Alpine	8	1,200	12,000	Feb. 17, 1875	$1 25	$20 00	9	April 8, 1874	$93,000		
Con. Amador		1,859	30,000							$210,000	
Bellevue	11	8,000	20,000	Feb. 17, 1875	50	50 00			111,000		
Calistoga		3,000	60,000								
Colerburg	2		24,000	Dec. 29, 1874	50		4	Feb. 6, 1873	24,000	24,000	
Chariot Mill	2	1,680	30,000	Feb. 17, 1875	50		4	Nov. 16, 1874	30,000	51,000	
Eureka			20,000				76	Dec. 8, 1873		2,094,000	
Gonsseo Valley											
Independent	8	1,800	25,000	March 18, 1875	50	6 93			95,500		
Keystone Quartz			10,000				10	Feb. 10, 1874		5,000	
Magenta	1	1,900	20,000	June 27, 1874	50				10,000		
Mansfield		3,300	66,000								
St. Patrick	10	1,800	20,000	Feb. 2, 1875	50				160,000		
Wonder Con											
Wyoming Con											
Yulo Gravel	5	400	10,000	Nov. 9, 1874	10	5 00	9	April 10, 1872	9,000	40,000	
									$594,500	$2,434,000	

WASHOE MINES.

COMPANIES.	No. Ass't in Mine	No. Ft. in Mine	No. Shares in Mine.	Last Assessment Levied.	Am't per Sh	Am't per Ft	No. D'v'ds	Last Dividend.	Total Am't Ass's Levied	Total Am't Div'ds Dis'd	Remarks.
Alamo	1	3,000	30,000	Nov. 2, 1872	$0 25				$ 7,500		
American Flat South		1,200	48,059								
Alpha Con	6	300	30,000	Nov. 11, 1873	3 00	$60 00			150,000		
Alta	1	1,800	36,000	Nov. 20, 1873	10				3,600		
American Flat	6	1,018	30,000	Feb. 8, 1875	2 00				135,000		
Andes	4	1,000	50,000	Feb. 25, 1875	1 50	25 00			150,000		
Bacon M. & M. Co	3	65	25,000	March 9, 1876	50				12,500		
Baltimore Con	7	2,632	54,000	Dec. 5, 1874	1 00				351,000		
Beach & Paxton			60,000								
Best & Belcher	9	540	100,800	July 13, 1874	50	8 00			136,192		
Belcher	8	1,040	104,000	April 14, 1871	4 00	40 00	33	Dec. 10, 1874	660,400	$14,135,000	
Bowers		20	5,000								
Bullion	45	943¾	100,000	Aug. 6, 1872	1 50	15 00			1,802,000		
Buckeye	13	3,000	48,000	March 4, 1875	50				242,000		
Caledonia	11	2,188	30,000	March 9, 1875	3 00	12 00			680,000		
California		600	540,000								
Central Comstock		2,000	60,000								
Challenge Con		90	60,000								
Chollar-Potosi	5	1,400	28,000	Nov. 14, 1874	5 00	50 00	39	Feb. 10, 1872	742,000	3,080,000	
Comstock		750	100,000								
Confidence	10	130	24,960	March 18, 1873	1 00	36 00	6	May 1, 1865.	243,260	78,000	
Con. Virginia	15	710	108,000	June 11, 1873	3 00	60 00	11	Apr. 11, 1875	411,200	5,360,000	
Con. Gold Hill Quartz	1	21	20,000	Aug. 4, 1873	75						
Con. Washoe		1,200	40,000								
Cosmopolitan		1,800	100,000								
Crown Point Ex		560	40,000								
Crown Point	21	680	100,000	Oct. 28, 1870	3 50	70 00	50	Jan. 12, 1875	622,370	11,588,000	
Crown Point Ravine	2	1,200	30,000	March 12, 1875	50	12 50			30,000		
Daney	12	2,000	24,000	Jan. 12, 1875	75	6 00	2	July 1, 1863	216,000	56,000	
Dayton	2	1,600	100,000	Feb. 16, 1875	1 00				200,000		
Dexter		1,200	60,000								
Dardanelles	2	1,260	60,000	Feb. 5, 1875	1 00	50 00			120,000		

Name							
Eclipse Winters Plato	1	35	25,000	Oct. 17, 1873	$ 50		
Empire Mill	17	70	50,000	Dec. 28, 1874	50		
Europa	2	1,000	20,000	July 14, 1874	25	$ 5 00	21
Exchequer	10	400	8,000	Feb. 3, 1874	3 00	60 00	
Fairmount		250	15,000				
Florida	1	1,300	60,000	Jan. 8, 1875	1 00		
Franklin		1,200	30,000				
Genowes		500	30,000				
Globe Con	6	4,300	38,000	March 18, 1875	75		
Georgia							
Gould & Curry	23	933½	108,000	Sept. 1, 1874	2 00	80 00	36
Green	1	1,634	20,000	Oct. 7, 1874	50		
Grenada		2,503	60,000				
Hale & Norcross	45	400	16,000	Jan. 8, 1875	5 00	200 00	36
Hartford		1,400	35,000				
Imperial	21	181	100,000	Feb. 10, 1875	1 00		
Independent & Omega		2,400	60,000				
Indus	3	950	30,000	June 10, 1868	25		30
Insurance	2	2,000	30,000	Dec. 10, 1874	10	1 50	
Julia	21	3,000	30,000	Sept. 13, 1873	2 00	30 00	
Justice	14	2,100	21,000	Feb. 12, 1875	3 00	30 00	
Kontuck	12	95	30,000	March 18, 1875	1 00		32
Knickerbocker	11	950	24,0.0	Dec. 3, 1874	1 50	30 00	
Kossuth	3	2,700	108,000	Dec. 28, 1874	50		
Lady Bryan	2	5,000	50,000	Feb. 25, 1875	50	5 00	
Lady Washington	2	1,223	36,000	March 18, 1875	50		
Leo	3	1,600	32,000	Dec. 23, 1874	50	5 00	
Lower Comstock		2,800	86,000	June 8, 1874			
Mexican	1	600	108,000	March 22, 1875	50		
Midas		200	30,000				
Mint	9	1,300	50,000	Jan. 19, 1875	20		
Nevada		800	40,000				
New York	12	3,000	36,000	Feb. 16, 1875	50	10 00	
Niagara		1,500	100,000				
North Carson		1,500	60,000				
North Utah		1,600	40,000				
Occidental	3	1,706	30,000	Feb. 2, 1875	50		
Or Gold Hill	2	1,400	30,000	Dec. 12, 1874	50	72 00	
Ophir	28	675	100,00	Feb. 19, 1874	1 00		22
Overman	31	1,00	38,400	March 16, 1875	3 00		

	$ 12,500	
May 16, 1867	416,400	712,500
	10,000	
	180,000	
	50,000	
	142,500	
Oct. 10, 1870	1,532,000	3,826,800
	10,000	
Apr. 10, 1871	1,550,000	1,528,000
	1,370,000	1,067,500
June 10, 1868		
	13,500	
	10,500	
	488,700	
	599,500	
	270,000	
Mar. 10, 1870	276,000	1,252,000
	108,000	
	175,000	
	36,000	
	27,200	
	51,000	
	50,000	
	225,000	
	10,000	
	62,500	
	30,000	
Mar. 9, 1864	1,982,800	1,394,400
	1,046,280	

WASHOE MINES—Continued.

COMPANIES.	No. Ass't	No. Ft. in Mine	No. Shares in Mine	Last Assessment Levied.	Am't per Sh	Am't per Ft	No. D'vds	Last Dividend.	Total Am't Ass's Levied	Total Am't Div'ds Dis'd	Remarks.
Pacific	..	1,200	48,000	..	..	..	..	..	..	..	
Patten	..	1,000	50,000	Feb. 3, 1875	$ 20	..	..	..	$ 10,000	..	
Phil Sheridan	2	1,200	24,000	Jan. 27, 1875	75	$10 00	..	..	30,000	..	
Pictou	7	2,0 0	30,000	March 2, 1875	25	3 75	..	..	45,700	..	
Rock Island	7	1,200	24,000	March 11, 1875	1 00	..	..	..	156,000	..	
Savage	17	771	16,000	Feb. 19, 1875	5 00	100 00	52	June 11, 1869	1,834,000	4,460,000	
Seg. Belcher	14	160	6,400	July 20, 1871	5 00	200 00	..	..	212,800	..	
Senator	11	2,000	24,000	Feb. 25, 1875	50	..	..	..	87,500	..	
Seg. Caledonia	..	100	10,000	June 22, 1874	10	..	..	..	1,000	..	
Seg. Rock Island	2	600	60,000	..	..	..	..	..	..	..	
South Comstock	1	1,636	40,000	Aug. 18, 1874	50	10 00	..	..	20,000	..	
South Justice	..	..	..	..	..	..	..	..	..	..	
South Overman	1	2,000	30,000	April 4, 1874	50	..	..	..	15,000	..	
South Star	..	1,200	48,000	..	..	..	..	..	..	..	
Sutro	2	2,400	24,000	Feb. 17, 1875	50	..	..	..	24,000	..	
Silver Central Con	..	1,500	110,000	..	..	..	..	..	..	..	
Silver Cloud	1	3,000	32,000	March 19, 1874	25	..	..	..	8,000	..	
Silver Hill	5	3,073	64,000	Feb. 16, 1875	2 00	..	..	..	540,000	..	
Sierra Nevada	40	2,640	100,000	Dec. 14, 1874	1 00	8 00	11	Jan. 16, 1871	810,000	102,600	
Huscor M. & M.	10	2,410	68,400	Nov. 27, 1874	1 00	..	2	Oct. 16, 1871	273,900	22,800	
Trench	1	20	5,000	Oct. 17, 1873	1 00	..	..	..	5,000	..	
Tyler	7	2,200	33,000	Nov. 19, 1874	50	4 50	..	..	62,700	..	
Union Consolid	7	803	100,000	Feb. 6, 1875	50	..	..	..	110,000	..	
Utah	9	1,000	20,000	March 19, 1875	2 00	40 00	..	..	180,000	..	
Ward	..	532	40,000	..	..	..	..	..	..	..	
Wells Fargo	2	1,500	36,000	March 17, 1875	10	2 40	..	..	7,200	..	
Whitman	..	1,800	100,000	..	..	..	..	..	..	..	
Woodville	8	1,700	120,000	Nov. 9, 1874	1 00	20 00	..	..	249,000	..	
Yellow Jacket	19	957	24,000	Dec. 10, 1874	5 00	100 00	25	Aug. 10, 1871	2,118,000	2,184,000	
									$24,649,302	$19,858,500	

WHITE PINE.

Companies.	No. Ass't in Mine	No. Ft. in Mine	No. Shares in Mine	Last Assessment Levied.	Am't per Sh	Am't per Ft D'vds	No. D'vds	Last Dividend.	Total Am't Ass'm Levied	Total Am't Div'ds Dis'd	Remarks.
General Lee	6	1,000		20,000	Jan. 9, 1873	$0 25	$2 00			$15,000		
Hayes	6	1,000		40,000	Jan. 4, 1875	20	12 00			59,400		
Mammoth	18	1,800		36,000	Feb. 25, 1875	50	2 00			99,000		
Or. Hidden Treas	11		21,333	Oct. 12, 1874	1 00		1	June 10, 1874	330,061	$31,999	
Silver Wave	11	1,600		20,000	Sept. 20, 1873	40	5 12			160,000		
									$658,461	$31,999	

IDAHO.

Companies.	No. Ass't in Mine	No. Ft. in Mine	No. Shares in Mine	Last Assessment Levied.	Am't per Sh	Am't per Ft D'vds	No. D'vds	Last Dividend.	Total Am't Ass's Levied	Total Am't Div'ds Dis'd	Remarks.
Empire	9			25,000	Jan. 30, 1875	$1 00				$275,000		
Golden Chariot	13	750		30,000	March 8, 1875	2 00		13	Oct. 24, 1873	615,000	$500,000	
Ida Ellmoro	16			30,000	Feb. 1, 1875	1 00		6	Feb. 8, 1870	656,000	60,000	
Mahogany	15	720		25,000	Jan. 5, 1875	2 00	$62 08	1	Aug. 5, 1872	140,000	15,000	
Poorman	2			50,000	Jun. 19, 1875	1 00				50,000		
Silver Cord	8			24,000	Feb. 27, 1875	1 00				126,000		
South Chariot	12	660		50,000	Jan. 9, 1875	1 00				275,000		
Virtue	4	2,500		20,000	Jan. 20, 1874	1 00	5 00			120,000		
War Eagle	9	1,000		10,000	Jan. 25, 1875	1 00				110,000		
Red Jacket	6	1.00		20,000	Feb. 1, 1875	50	12 25			100,000		
										$2,652,000	$575,000	

COPE DISTRICT.

COMPANIES.	No. Ass't in Mine.	No. Ft. in Mine	No. Shares in Mine.	Last Assessment Levied.	Am't per Sh	Am't per Ft	No. D'vds	Last Dividend.	Total Am't Ass's Levied	Total Am't Div'ds Dis'd	Remarks.
Excelsior	1		12,000	June 20, 1872.	$2 00				$ 24,000		

ELY DISTRICT.

COMPANIES.	No. Ass't in Mine.	No. Ft. in Mine	No. Shares in Mine.	Last Assessment Levied.	Am't per Sh	Am't per Ft	No. D'vds	Last Dividend.	Total Am't Ass's Levied	Total Am't Div'ds Dis'd	Remarks.
Amador Tunnel	2	3,000	30,000	Feb. 5, 1874	$1 00	$30 00			$ 60,000		
American Flag	6		30,000	Nov. 10, 1874	50				195,000		
Alps	8	800	30,000	Feb. 10, 1875	25				105,000		
Bowery	6		30,000	Dec. 15, 1874	20				94,500		
Charter Oak	3	1,000	30,000	Jan. 9, 1874	50	15 00			30,000		
Chapman	4		30,000	July 28, 1873	25				37,500		
Cherry Creek	2	1,600	30,000	Feb. 17, 1875	35				15,000		
Chief of the Hill	5		30,000	Aug. 11, 1874	25				67,500		
Condor	3		25,000	July 17, 1874	25				37,500		
Huhn & Hunt	10	3,600	30,000	Sept. 24, 1874	30				279,000		
Ingomar	7	1,000	40,000	May 4, 1874	25	10 00			70,000		
Louise	3	2,400	30,000	Sept. 15, 1872	50						
Meadow Valley	8		60,000	Feb. 11, 1875	1 00		17	June 16, 1873	270,000	$1,200,000	
Newark	10	800	32,000	Feb. 2, 1875	1 00	80 00			288,600		
Pacific Tunnel		1,250	30,000								
Page & Panaca	8	2,400	40,000	Oct. 6, 1874	75				190,000		
Pinto		23,000	50,000								
Pioche	8	1,000	20,000	Dec. 11, 1874	1 00	20 00	3	Aug. 5, 1872	180,000	60,000	
Pioche Phenix	3		40,000	May 6, 1873	1 00				100,000		
Pioche West Ex	7		35,000	March 10, 1875	1 00				101,500		
Portland	5		30,000	Aug. 21, 1874	25				71,000		
Raymond & Ely	3	5,000	30,000	Jan. 18, 1875	3 00	18 00	23	Sept. 10, 1873	220,000	3,075,000	
Rye Patch	3	1,000	30,000	July 21, 1874	25		4	Mar. 5, 1875	67,500	37,000	
Silver Peak	5		30,000	Sept. 3, 1874	50				90,000		
Silver West Con	1		50,000	June 10, 1873	75				37,500		

ELY DISTRICT—Continued.

COMPANIES.	No. As't in Mine	No. Ft. in Mine	No. Shares in Mine.	Last Assessment Levied.	Am't per Sh	Am't per Ft	No. D'vds	Last Dividend.	Total Am't Ass's Levied	Total Am't Div'ds Dis'd	Remarks.
Stanvland	1	800	30,000	May 16, 1873	$2 00				$60,000		
Spring Mount	3		35,000	May 14, 1873	50				43,750		
Spring Mountain Tun	9		20,000	May 22, 1874	20				33,040		
Wash. & Creole	14	1,520	30,000	Feb. 18, 1875	1 00	$75 00			292,600		
Watson	1		30,000	Nov. 16, 1874	1 00				30,000		
Webfoot	1		50,000	Jan. 23, 1875	25				12,500		
Yellow Stone		1,000	30,000								
									$3,348,700	$4,365,000	

UTAH.

COMPANIES.	No. As't in Mine	No. Ft. in Mine	No. Shares in Mine.	Last Assessment Levied.	Am't per Sh	Am't per Ft	No. D'vds	Last Dividend.	Total Am't Ass's Levied	Total Am't Div'ds Dis'd	Remarks.
Wellington	4		50,000	Feb. 17, 1874	$0 25				$ 55,000		

EUREKA DISTRICT.

COMPANIES.	No. As't in Mine	No. Ft. in Mine	No. Shares in Mine.	Last Assessment Levied.	Am't per Sh	Am't per Ft	No. D'vds	Last Dividend.	Total Am't Ass's Levied	Total Am't Div'ds Dis'd	Remarks.
Adams Hill	6		50,000	Feb. 16, 1875	$0 15				$57,500		
Columbus	3		50,000	Nov. 26, 1873	50				87,500		
Eureka Con			50,000				17	Mar. 5, 1875		$725,000	
Jackson	6		50,000	June 25, 1873	10				62,500		
K. K. Con			60,000				4	Sept.15, 1873		60,000	
Phenix	14		50,000	April 21, 1874	50				337,500		
Star Consolidated	3	18,000	50,000	June 19, 1873	10				30,000		
									$665,500	$750,000	

PHILADELPHIA.

COMPANIES.	No. As't in Mine	No. Ft. in Mine	No. Shares in Mine.	Last Assessment Levied.	Am't per Sh	Am't per Ft	No. D'v'ds	Last Dividend.	Total Am't Ass's Levied	Total Am't Div'ds Dis'd	Remarks.
Belmont	4		50,000	Oct. 9, 1874	$1 00				$225,000		
El Dorado North	1		25,000	Aug. 4, 1874	50				12,500		
El Dorado South Con.	5	2,000	40,000	Jan. 15, 1875	75				237,500		
Josephine	1		25,000	July 10, 1874	15				3,750		
North Belmont	2		50,000	Sept. 30, 1874	10				10,000		
Prussian	3			Jan. 12, 1875	1 00	$5 00					
Quntero	3	2,000	50,000	Sept. 30, 1874	10				15,000	$75,000	
Monitor Belmont	4	6,400	50,000	March 16, 1875	50		3	Dec. 5, 1873	100,000		
									$713,750	$75,000	

ESMERALDA DISTRICT.

COMPANIES.	No. As't in Mine	No. Ft. in Mine	No. Shares in Mine.	Last Assessment Levied.	Am't per Sh	Am't per Ft	No. D'v'ds	Last Dividend.	Total Am't Ass's Levied	Total Am't Div'ds Dis'd	Remarks.
Juniata Consolidated	2	5,000	50,000	Dec. 16, 1874	$1 00	$6 50			$82,500		

Total amount of assessments levied upon stocks dealt in the S. F. Stock and Exchange Board.. $33,468,413
Total amount dividends paid upon stocks dealt in the S. F. Stock and Exchange Board........ $58,089,499

STOCK AND MONEY BROKERS,

SAN FRANCISCO.

Abbott O, stocks, 302 Sansome
Ainsworth A G, Cal Stock and Exchange Board
Armstrong J L, stock, 422 Montgomery
Baird Andrew, money, 316 California
Baldridge J E, stocks, 404 Montgomery
Baldridge M, stocks, 404 Montgomery
Baldwin E J, 509 California
Banks T C, money, 14 Merchants' Exchange
Barris Layerne, 302 Montgomery
Barton William H, 411½ California
Bear S, money 140 Montgomery
Benjamin M H, stocks, 430 Montgomery
Berggren Aug, money, 406 Montgomery
Blair T M, sergeant-at-arms S F Stock Exchange Board, 411½ California
Blake W, stock, 405½ Montgomery
Bogart J M, stocks, 402 Montgomery
Bourne J B, stocks, 400 California
Brooks & Lee, stocks, 415 Montgomery
Brown J W, stock, 408 California
Budd W C, stocks, 440 California
Burling & Bro., stocks, 323 California
Burtsell J M, stocks, 106 Leidesdorff
Cantin & Everett, stocks, 313 California
Cahill E & Co., stocks, 406 Montgomery
Callaghan, Lynch & Co., stocks, 110 Leidesdorff
Cavallier Julius, stocks, 513 California
Cheesman, Head & Thornburg, stocks, 412 Montgomery
Child & Maguire, stock, Merchants' Exchange
Cogan James, money, 317 California
Cohn & Frank, money 418 Montgomery
Coleman John W, stock, 435 California
Cope, Uhler & Co., stock, 503 California
Coursen G A, stocks, 432 Montgomery
Crocker J H, stocks, 215 Sansome
Crosby F W, stocks, 432 Montgomery
Cumming John, stocks, 402 Mantgomery
David Jules, 408 Battery
Davidson J, money, 311 Battery
Deane Coll, stock, 311 California
De Greayer S, stocks, 422 Montgomery
De Pass J M, 331 Montgomery
Dixon Samuel, stocks, 501 California

Duncan Wm L, stocks, 424 Montgomery
Duncan Wm T, 405 California
Ehrlich & Steinhart, stocks, 413 California
Elliott Richard, stocks, 45 Merchants' Exchange
Eyre E E, stocks, 424 Montgomery
Farnham Edward, 434 Montgomery
Fay Philip S, money, 420 Montgomery
Fay T J, 420 Montgomery
Fernald J S, 426 California
Finlayson James R, 534 California
Fisk Asa, note, 240 Montgomery
Fitch J R, stocks, 411½ California
Flagg H H, stocks, 420 Montgomery
Ford & Fuller, stocks, 420 Montgomery
Fox Chas W, stocks, 408 Montgomery
Franks Fred, stocks, 331 Montgomery
Fry Edward M, 116 Leidesdorff
Fuhr Charles A, 208 Montgomery
Gardenhire W C, 418 California
Gautier E, 424 Montgomery
Gedge J H P, 323 Montgomery
Gillon James, 408 Montgomery
Gladwin Geo S, money, 410½ California
Glassman J, money, 335 Montgomery
Glazier I & Co, stocks 412 California
Glover G F M, stock, 430 California
Goldsmith Bros, 108 Sansome
Green & Hendrie, stocks, 418 Montgomery
Greenbaum L, money, 306 Montgomery
Grim A K, stocks, 331 Montgomery
Hall & Charles, stocks and bullion, 408 Mont
Hagan & Manheim, 316 California
Hall Edward F & Co, stocks, 410 California
Hassey F A, stocks, 402 Montgomery
Harvey Chas C, stock, 8 Leidesdorff
Hawkins J J E, stock, 306 Montgomery
Henriques David, stocks, 432 Montgomery
Herr J J, stock, 422 Montgomery
Higgins & Conkling, stocks, 13 Merchants' Exch
Higgins Edward & Co, 406 California
Hill & Kilgour, stock, 403 California
Himmelman A, money, 637 Washington
Hoag Jared C, stocks, 200 Davis
Hoare C W, stock, 420 Montgomery
Hoitt Ira G, money, 421 Montgomery
Holmes A & Co, money, ne cor Clay and Mont
Holt Z, stocks, 330 Pine
Hopkins & Haley, money, 410½ California
Hopkins C H, stocks, 434 Montgomery
Hosmer & Bourne, 113 Leidesdorff
Howard H C, stocks, 422 Montgomery
Hubbard & Johnson, 319 California
Hull M J, money, 206 Montgomery
Hunt J L, stock, 12 Stevenson Building

Hussey J L, stocks, 421 Montgomery
Ives George I, stocks, 402 Montgomery
Jacobs M I & Co, money, 238 Montgomery
Jones F, 728 Market
Jones J H & Co, stocks, 509 California
Jones W A & Co, money, 238 Montgomery
Kemm Joseph, general, 24 Montgomery Block
Kenney Charles A, stocks, 411 California
King, J L, 434 California
Kinsey A, stocks, 108 Leidesdorff
Klopenstine J, stocks, 422 Montgomery
Klumpke J G, stocks, 432 Montgomery
Knox & Lissak, stocks, 409 California
Kreider Frank L, stock, r 19, 330 Pine
Kreider S D, 330 Pine
Latham James H & Co, money and stocks, 411 California
Levy Jacob & Co, money, 420 Montgomery
Lincoln Jonas, stocks, 329 Montgomery
Lissak A H Jr, 409 California
Little John T, money, 405½ California
Loveland L F, stocks, 418 California
Luty F E, stocks, 507 Montgomery
Mahoney J H, stocks, 418 Montgomery
Marks Edmond, general, 418 Montgomery
Martin M S, stocks, 411½ California
McCombe John, money, 507 Montgomery
McDonald Mark L, stocks, 513 California
McDonald M J, stocks, 215 Sansome
McHaffie Jas, stocks, 408 California
Menn J H, money, 522 Montgomery
Merzbach Julius, money, 530 Montgomery
Meyer Daniel, money, 212 Pine
Meyer Jonas, money, 212 Pine
Meyer Matthias, money, 212 Pine
Miles Paul, stocks, 606 Montgomery
Miller George, stocks, 411 California
Mohrhardt P F, stocks, 411½ California
Montealegre J Gerard, money, 329 Montgomery
Moore J M, stocks, 422 Montgomery
Moritz M, money, 329 Montgomery
Moulder & Vimont, stocks, 308 Sansome
Newburger E & Co, money, 432 Montgomery
Noble H H & Co, 435 California
Noyes C G, stocks, 430 California
O'Connor Thos, money, 512 Montgomery
Page R C & Co, stocks, 405½ California
Parker & Fry, stocks, 112 Leidesdorff
Parker James M, 609 Sacramento
Parker J D, 304 Montgomery
Parmelee George E, 424 Montgomery
Peckerman E L, 413 California
Peckham E P, stocks, 413 California
Peltret Peter G, money, 317 Battery

Perry J Jr, stocks, 104 Leidesdorff
Peyser Herman, 719 Montgomery
Poulterer T J, stocks, 409 California
Purdy, Van Brunt & Robbins, 405 California,
Rawson J A, money, 605 Clay
Reuben Henry, 222 Montgomery
Reynolds Wm T, stocks, 111½ Leidesdorff
Rich David, stock, 422 Montgomery
Richon N, money, 611 Commercial
Robbins E V, stocks, 413 California
Rogers Robert F, stocks, 331 Montgomery
Romero & Aguirre, money, 500 Kearny
Rose L S, stocks, 415 Montgomery
Ruppin B, money, 222 Montgomery
Ruply R, money, 607 Clay
Salomon J, money, 502 Kearny
Sanborn T C, stocks, 409 California
Schmiedell, Hochstadter & Co, stocks, 401 California
Schmitt B L, stocks, 6 Merchants' Exchange
Schmitt J L, money, 6 Merchants' Exchange
Shawhan J E, stocks, 432 Montgomery
Sherwood B F & Co, stocks, 406½ California
Shotwell J M, stocks, 302 Sansome
Smiley Geo W, stocks, 444 California
Smiley Joseph E, 236 Montgomery
Smiley T J L, stocks, prest Cal S E Board, 423 California
Smith E L, stocks, 302 Montgomery
Smith W J, stocks, Cal Stock Exchange Board
Snowball R Y, stocks, 106 Leidesdorff
Soren G S, stocks, Cal Stock Exch Board
Stark John, stocks, 411½ California
Stoutenborough & Hall, stocks, 401 California
Sutro Charles, money, 415 Montgomery
Sutro Gustav, money, 415 Montgomery
Sweet H A, stocks, 236 Montgomery
Taylor W S, stocks, 420 Montgomery
Turnbull Walter & Co, stocks, 410½ California
Twing D H & Co, money, 404 Montgomery
Vinzent C, stocks, 424 Montgomery
Viot Eugene, stocks, 446 California
Webster & Smith, money, 310 Montgomery
Weihe Aug, money, 400 Montgomery
Wilder H, money, 626 Montgomery
Wilke F E, stocks, 411 California
Winans J C, stocks, 319 California
Wiswell Thaddeus, money, 626 Montgomery
Wolf F, stocks, 424 Montgomery
Wood H P, stocks, 331 Montgomery
Wood John, stock, 64 Merchants' Exchange
Woods & Freeborn, stocks, 317 California
Wright W H, stocks, 420 Montgomery
Zinns L A, stocks, 106 Leidesdorff

PANAMINT MINING DISTRICT.

Inyo Co., California.

Since the original discoveries of rich mineral districts in the mountains of California and the Territories, no one has been of greater extent than the new district of Panamint, or has made as good a showing for so short a time. The heretofore great isolation of this country from the more settled portions of the country; its apparent sterility and barrenness, together with the terrible stories that were told of the fearful neighborhood of "dry lakes" and "Death Valley," kept people away from it. But the discoveries recently made there of immense lodes of silver has suddenly changed these mountains from abodes of silence to teeming life and activity. The following from the *Evening Post* of April 3, 1875, is quoted, which gives in detail the observations of one of the editorial staff of that paper who has returned from a trip made to the new district, who tells all about the matter. He says:

"In 1862, Washoe was a long way from San Francisco. Virginia City has since become one of its suburbs. Panamint twelve months ago was a *terra incognita*; in a year or two it will be a southern suburb, as Virginia City is an Eastern one. The Comstock has been an active agency in building up this town. In 1877, if not before, Panamint will be an equal partner in the business, and will do her fair share of labor in carrying on the work of enlarging and beautifying the metropolis of the Pacific. The Comstock has had its Crown Point and Belcher, and is now breaking into the crust of its great bonanza, and drifts and winzes and diamond drills show hundreds of millions of dollars in sight. Panamint, with far less work, shows hardly less results. The Comstock wealth, by hard and persistent labor, after years of anxious expenditure, is found 1,500 to 2,000 feet below the surface. Panamint already vies with it ton for ton and assay for assay, though its deepest shafts and longest tunnels are not much over three hundred feet. With this preamble your eye witness will proceed at once to introduce such testimony as he has to support these somewhat extraordinary statements.

"THE WYOMING GROUP.

"The Wyoming Consolidated Company is working among others the following leading mines, and your own witness, from his own measurements and examinations, records these results: The Wyoming Mine has, by shafts and tunnels, been explored to a depth of 315 feet below the croppings. At the croppings is an open cut of 75 feet long and 25 feet in depth. At this point the vein is in slate. From the hill-side and at a depth from the floor of the cutting of 85 feet vertical, a tunnel has been run in eastwardly on the vein for a distance of 160 feet, and shows a well defined ledge of a width of 5 to 6 feet, with pay ore from wall to wall. The mountain in which the Wyoming is located is capped with a strata of slate for 150 feet in height. The cutting and tunnel hitherto spoken of are in this slate. But the vein carries the same character through and below the slate into the limestone formation. At the greater depth of 177 feet below the croppings, or 67 feet below the floor of the before mentioned tunnel, a second tunnel has been run from the east side of the mountain westwardly on the vein a distance of 164 feet, showing a well-defined ledge from 5 to 6 feet, with pay ore from wall to wall. On the west side of this mountain, 192 feet below the croppings, or 15 feet below the second tunnel, a third has been run in on the vein eastwardly a distance of 125 feet. This tunnel is in limestone, and shows a well-defined vein of full 6 feet in width, with pay ore from wall to wall. At a depth of 285 feet below the surface, or 95 feet below the third tunnel, a fourth tunnel has been run in from the west side, going diagonally in a general easterly direction, and has struck the front ledge at a distance of 154 feet. In a former communication describing the Wyoming claim, it was mentioned that there was a spur running for 450 feet at the westward end of the ledge, giving it somewhat the form of the lettet Y. In addition to the open cut on the croppings of the main vein, a cut of 300 feet in length and from 10 to 15 feet in depth has been made on the spur, or front vein. In this open cut the vein is 3 to 4 feet in width, and a large quantity of high grade ore has been taken out. The front vein at the point at which it is intersected by the last mentioned tunnel is 6 feet in width, and shows high pay ore for 4 feet of that width. The point at which this tunnel meets the front ledge is 100 feet below the surface. The tunnel has been continued 25 feet further, and strikes the main ledge, and at this point the back ledge is fully 7 feet in width, well defined, and has pay ore from wall to wall. This shows a paying ledge on the main vein 285 feet from the floor of the lowest tunnel to the croppings. The front ledge, from these developments, is seen to be 450 feet long, and with an ascertained average depth from surface to tunnel floor of 100 feet. Both veins, as exposed by the lowest workings, are richer and lie between even better defined walls than in the higher levels, showing that so far from growing weaker as they descend both are stronger, and are unquestionably true fissure veins.

THE MARVEL

Is a continuation of the Wyoming mine and at the west end of the vein. This mine is the property of the Wyoming Consolidated Company. But little work has been done on it, although the croppings are larger and extend the entire length of the claim, with indications of equal wealth below. The Marvel, from its eastern boundary (next the Wyoming) for 200 feet westward, shows enormous croppings from 20 to 40 feet wide and standing up against the hill-side like a great retaining wall of masonry, and 25 feet in height. From all appearances the Marvel is one of the most promising of this company's mines, though little work has been performed in developing it beyond what nature has done.

The Hemlock—also the property of the Wyoming Company—is situated about 3,000 feet from the Wyoming. On the croppings there is an open cut of 350 feet in length and an average of 20 feet in depth. From the floor of this cut a winze has been sunk to a depth of 80 feet, following the ledge, all the way in high grade ore. On the surface the vein averages 3 feet, and at the bottom of the winze it is fully 5 feet wide, a well-defined ledge, with high grade ore from wall to wall. Drifts have been run laterally east and west from the bottom of this winze 50 feet each way, showing a strong vein of good ore. On the east end of the vein, at the vertical depth of 150 feet below the croppings, a tunnel has been started from the mountain side and run in 75 feet on the vein westwardly, showing a well-defined and strong ledge all the way. Near the west end of the ledge a tunnel has been run from the face of the mountain, striking the vein at right angles at 100 feet from the mouth and the same distance below the croppings. From this point a drift has been run on the vein eastwardly 150 feet and another westwardly 50 feet. These show for 200 feet a well defined and unbroken ledge 6 feet wide and carrying high grade ore from wall to wall. From the floor of this tunnel, at its intersection of the ledge, a winze has been sunk a depth of 104 feet on the vein. At the bottom of this winze, or 204 feet below the croppings, the vein is found to be 9 feet in width, with 5 feet of pay streak between its well-defined walls. The vein seems to be growing stronger and wider as depth is attained. Further to explore this vein, when the winze had reached a depth of 50 feet below the tunnel, drifts were run on the vein 40 feet each way, and showed the best ore yet found in the mine. Large bodies of ore ready for stoping have been developed by work done on this property.

The Alabama (another of the Wyoming Company's mines) is unquestionably an extension of the Hemlock lode. It has been developed by an open cut for a distance of 40 feet on the vein, reaching a depth of 30 feet below the croppings. From this point a tunnel has been run 75 feet on the vein, all the way yielding good ore and showing a width of 4 feet between well-defined walls. A winze has been sunk from near the end of the tunnel on the vein 80 feet in depth, and at the bottom 125 feet below the croppings; the ledge is 5 feet in width, yielding a very high grade ore. From the bottom of the winze a drift has been run eastwardly on the vein 40 feet, yielding from its entire length ore of high character. These developments show an enormous body of pay rock of great value.

The Esperanza (another of the Wyoming Company's mines) is opened by a shaft on the vein 40 feet deep, exposing a well-defined body of high grade ore. There are other mines belonging to the same company, on which less work has been done, but which give indications, from examination and assays of the croppings, of being hardly less valuable.

THE WONDER CONSOLIDATED COMPANY.

"This sister company consists of Jacobs' Wonder of the World, Stewart's Wonder, the Challenge, and Little Chief.

"The Jacobs' Wonder, or Wonder of the World—for it goes by both names—has been developed by an open cut running northerly from Jacobs' Gulch at right angles with the croppings, a distance of 50 feet, and continued by a tunnel 25 feet further until it strikes the ledge. From the point of intersection tunnels have been run east and west on the vein. The easterly tunnel is 225 feet long. In places the ledge is from 12 to 15 feet wide, with an average of 8 feet vein matter and 6 feet of pay ore. The westerly tunnel has been driven 200 feet, and the vein on that side is equally large and strong. This claim is 1,500 feet long, and is cut about the center by the gulch. From the cropping on the west side to the level of the floor of the tunnel is 330 feet. The croppings are bold from the bottom of the gulch to the summit, and are from 10 to 20 feet in width. This shows an immense body of ore lying between the tunnel floor and the surface on this portion of the mine. On the other side, east from the gulch 350 feet, a shaft has been sunk 110 feet on the vein to the level of the east tunnel. It shows at the bottom a ledge of full 7 feet in width with good walls, and 5 feet of pay ore. The vein in this shaft is continuous from top to bottom, and grows stronger as it descends. This is conclusive evidence that the vein carries the same general features not only between the tunnel and the shaft, but to the boundary of the claim. Two winzes have been sunk from the croppings on the vein between the shaft and the intersecting gulch, one 50 feet and the other 60 feet in depth; and drifts have been run from the bottom of each winze each way, and connecting the two winzes, and showing a vein from 12 to 14 feet in width with 7 feet of pay ore.

" Joining the Jacobs' Wonder at its eastern boundary is the Challenge, a mine with 750 feet of ground. It extends to the western boundary of the Stewart's Wonder. The Challenge is developed by a tunnel run on the vein westwardly a distance of 100 feet, showing a well-defined ledge the whole distance. The croppings show large and bold from the Stewart's Gulch on the east of the summit. The distance from the level of the tunnel floor to the upper croppings is 275 feet.

"Stewart's Wonder (the next mine on the east and on the same vein as the Challenge and Wonder of the World) is developed by a tunnel started from the bottom of Stewart's Gulch, at the boundary of the Challenge, running eastwardly on the vein. This tunnel has a length of 125 feet, showing a well-defined and good vein of from 5 to 7 feet in width. At a vertical height of 125 feet above this tunnel, another tunnel has been driven in the same direction 175 feet. This tunnel—like the one below—shows a well-defined vein, but of 4 to 5 feet width of good paying ore. Besides this second tunnel, and at 115 feet vertical above it, a third tunnel has been driven in 225 feet on the vein, showing a continuous body of 4 feet width of pay ore. At a point still higher and at a 100 feet from the mouth of the third tunnel, a winze has been sunk on the ledge from the surface, reaching the tunnel at a depth of 75 feet. These developments expose a very large body of ore—the floor of the lower tunnel being 565 feet below the highest croppings.

"THE LITTLE CHIEF.

belonging to the Wonder Company, is located on the north side of Surprise Canyon and is very accessible to the company's mill. It is opened by a tunnel from a small side cañon, eastwardly on the vein a distance of 50 feet, and shows a well-defined high paying 3 foot vein the whole distance. Near the mouth of the tunnel a winze has been sunk 30 feet in depth on the vein, and it is found that at the bottom of this working the ledge has increased to 4 feet in width. The croppings are bold and large and running up the mountain on each side of the cañon several hundred feet. There has not been much artificial development of this mine, but what has been done by the company and by nature shows the existence of a large body of ore.

"ORE ON HAND AND IN SIGHT.

"The Wyoming Consolidated Company has on hand in its dumps 1,700 tons of average ore. This company, by careful measurements and exact calculations, made by your eye witness himself, has in sight between their lowest levels and the surface 102,000 tons of pay ore.

"The Wonder Consolidated Company has on its dumps 1,000 tons, averaging over $100 a ton. In sight, between their lowest workings and the surface, this company has 50,000 tons of ore. The expense of mining the ore now in sight in both companies and delivering it at the mills will be less than $10 a ton. The Wonder Company has a five-stamp mill, which, the steam power being sufficient, is now being enlarged to 10 stamps, and is running night and day crushing and concentrating; and will work up about 20 tons every 24 hours. The concentration apparatus used is known as the California Concentrator works by the wet process, and gives entire satisfaction. When the new stamps are at work the Wonder Company will be able to ship every day $1,200 to $1,500 worth of concentrated matter *en route*, for tide water. The ores of this company (as has been before stated) contain quite a large percentage of copper and are well adapted for concentration. This concentration system is so arranged that the slums can be saved and are well adapted for amalgamation in pans, as they contain chiefly chlorides and sulphurets of silver. This small mill will be run very profitably until a larger one more commensurate with the yield of the mines can be erected.

WHAT THE ASSAYS SHOW.

"The average of all the assays made up to this time—of ores from the mines of the Wonder Consolidated, and those assays are 113 in number—is $210.64 per ton. The assays run from $5 up to $1,200—the former being taken from vein matter which has not been considered in measuring up the pay ore in sight.

" The average of all assays made from ores from the mines of the Wyoming Consolidated Company — and whose assays number 351—is $337.43. These assays run from $10 to $2,000 per ton.

" The average of all assays made of Wyoming rock shows its value to be $337.43, but your eye witness, for the purpose of estimating the worth of the mines, will make a large allowance for all possible and improbable contingencies, and put the figure at $125 per ton.

"The average of all assays of the Wonder Consolidated mine is $210.61; but for the purposes of this calculation he will assume it to be less than one-half—or $100 per ton. These factors show the gross value of the ore mined and to be mined above the level of the present workings in the Wyoming mines to be $11,942,000, less the expense of milling; and the value of the ore in dump and in sight in the Wonder Consolidated mines to be $4,600,000.

"With the concentrating system now at work, and considering the indications of the freer character of the ore in the lower depths, it is probable that the companies will be able to mill up to 85 per cent.; but your eye witness' caution leads him to allow 30 per cent. for expenses and waste in milling, and this reduces the net product of bullion from the Wyoming mines now in sight to $8,358,850; and the net product of the Wonder mines to $3,220,000.

RECAPITULATION.

WYOMING CONSOLIDATED MINES.

Ore in dump, 1,700 tons at $125....................................	$ 212,500
Ore in sight, 102,000 tons at $125.................................	12,750,000
	$12,962,500
Mining 102,000 tons ore at $10 per ton...........................	1,020,000
	$11,942,500
Milling and loss at 30 per cent....................................	3,583,750
Net product..	$8,358,750

WONDER CONSOLIDATED MINES.

Ore in dump, 1,000 tons at $100....................................	$ 100,000
Ore in sight, 50,000 tons at $100...................................	5,000,000
	$5,100,000
Mining 50,000 tons at $10...	500,000
	$4,600,000
Milling and loss at 30 per cent....................................	$1,380,000
Net product..	$3,220,000

"In the beginning of this article your eye witness said he would establish the truth of his assertion, that Panamint would vie with the great Comstock in its results upon the prosperity of San Francisco by facts. The evidence in these statements, which are all based on actual inspection, guided by experienced knowledge and toned by caution and full recognition of all the risks of mining, makes argument unnecessary. Washoe, in 14 years, has done great things for this city; Panamint, in less than 12 months, promises as great results; and yet Panamint has cost up to this time less than $1,500,000. Your eye witness does not need to argue with a San Francisco community that the ledges of several mines that grow wider, stronger, richer and better defined as they are followed down are not likely to be accidentally cut off, pinched out, broken or suddenly impoverished at a few feet below the points which the drill and pick have hitherto reached. Nor does your eye witness need to argue with a San Francisco public that eight or ten mines, bought at one purchase by a few capitalists in a new, strange and little known country, embrace all the valuable mines in that district. That there are several mines in the district as valuable as the best of these he has mentioned is all but certain—that there are mines unprospected, perhaps unlocated, more valuable than any of them is not improbable. With what your eye witness has seen — and what your eye witness has good reasons for expecting from future explorations and discoveries—he, as a truthful, competent and prudent eye witness, claims that he has justified all that he has said about Panamint becoming the equal of the Comstock.

"The honor of creating this great source of wealth to California and in which the whole community will directly share — after due credit to the hardy prospectors who braved the dangers and endured the hardships of mountain and desert—belongs to Senators Jones and Stewart, T. W. Park and a few friends. Their reward must be great, and it will not have been like some fortunes by a happy operation in the stock market, but will be, the well earned result of a large investment, made on cool judgment and deliberate calculation. These men read the signs by which nature had marked the hiding place of one of the richest and most remarkable deposits of treasure. Money, knowledge and pluck are the keys which have unlocked the doors of a great vault of silver bullion."

The Sunday *Chronicle* of March 21, 1875, has a correspondence from the Panamint mines, in which the writer graphically describes the discovery of the Great Wonder Mine. We quote:

"THE PANAMINT MINES

"Were discovered some two years ago by R. C. Jacobs, Robert Stewart and William Kennedy, who were prospecting for mines in that vicinity. When crossing a divide, some two miles from the Wonder of the World, they could plainly see with their field-glasses across the cañon — over where Panamint City is now situated—the ledge, which showed as plainly as a wagon road, for some thousands of feet. When they crossed the cañon and prospected the ledge, which was bare, rising out of the mountain, they could scarcely believe their eyesight. There was an immense ledge, rich in native silver. This lode they named *The Wonder of the World*. Soon after this discovery they formed a mining district, and prospecting became general; and I venture to say that there never were so many valuable prospects for good mines found in any mining district in Nevada or California. The reports and ores brought in from this place to San Francisco soon attracted the attention of capitalists. Senators Jones and Stewart purchased the Wonder of the World, Stewart's Wonder, Challenge, and Little Chief, which are now incorporated, and the property of the Wonder Consolidated Mining Company. The Wonder of the World, after location and record, was divided into two claims, called after two of the discoverers, Jacobs and Stewart, and are now known as the Jacob's Wonder and Stewart's Wonder. These two mines are divided by a ravine, which necessitates a trail or road to each. The Jacob's Wonder has an immense ledge of ore. This mine is well opened, and work suspended, except in one or two places, they having so much ore in sight that they await the completion of the mills. This mine alone can furnish ore for a twenty-stamp mill for years to come. The Stewart's Wonder is an extension of the Jacob's Wonder; well opened, and in the same condition as the Jacob's Wonder, with more ore in sight than can be used for many months to come. These mines are on the left hand side of the ravine as you go up this cañon; the same as the Belcher and Crown Point at Gold Hill, Nevada."

LIST OF OFFICERS.

President.   Secretary.   Teasurer.
James A. Pritchard.   W. R. Townsend.   The Bank of California.

Trustees.
James A. Pritchard,   J. D. Fry,   B. Peart,   S. A. Raymond, Joseph McGillivray.

Office.
Rooms 1 and 2 Academy Building, 320 Pine Street, San Francisco,

THE CERRO GORDO MINING DISTRICT,

INYO COUNTY, CALIFORNIA.

WHAT ABOUT IT?

Why, it is a mountain half full of rich silver and lead ores!

Here are some fifteen well-known parallel veins of ore from thirty to one hundred feet wide, averaging one hundred dollars ($100.) per ton in silver, and sixty per cent. of lead, within the space of 4,000 feet lineal distance.

It has sent more than five millions of dollars ($5,000,000) in bullion to San Francisco in the last six years, at an outlay of one hundred thousand dollars ($100,000.) It is capable of furnishing with ease, ten millions of dollars ($10,000,000.) annually.

It supplies the Selby Refining Works in San Francisco, with a large part of their bullion. It is

THE OBJECTIVE POINT

of the Los ANGELES and CERRO GORDO RAILROAD, now pushing forward with the greatest energy, and in connection with Panamint, will put Inyo in the front rank of mining counties.

It is no half tried experiment. It has been worked six years, and with no proper facilities. The miners have gone down 750 feet into the bowels of the mountain, and find the veins wider and richer as they go.

For months together it has kept one hundred 12 mule teams busy hauling out bullion to Los Angeles.

It can furnish bullion freight enough to make the Cerro Gordo Railroad a paying investment.

WHAT ARE SOME OF THE PRINCIPAL MINES?

The Union, down 750 feet with a 40 foot vein, worth $2,000,000; the Omega, vein 30 feet wide; Santa Maria, vein 100 feet wide; Ignacio Silver mine, ore averages one hundred and eighty dollars ($180.) per ton, runs to $1,800; Jefferson, Carman, Guadaloupe, Guymas, First and Second Lead Mines, San Benito, Alpha, and farthest in the series the Buena Vista, cropping one hundred feet wide on the summit of the mountain.

WHAT CLASS OF ORES?

Smelting ores of the finest kind: Argentiferous Galena, Sulphurets, Carbonates, Sulphates, and Chlorides. Silver Sulphurates and Chlorides. A thirty inch Cupola furnace eight feet high, runs out a pig of bullion weighing eighty-five pounds every six minutes throughout the twenty-four hours, and does this one hundred days in succession without cooling off.

Raymond the U. S. Commissioner on mining statistics, expresses his surprise at the furnace work at Cerro Gordo, and says "It is the pride of these works that they smelt more ore with less fuel than any other works in the country." He gives comparative statistics showing that they use less than half as much fuel as some of the celebrated furnaces in Europe. The charges are made up of Galena ores, Carbonates and Quartzose silver ores, with the proper quantity of ferruginous ores.

HOW ABOUT TITLES?

They are clean and undisputed.

WELL WHAT IS THE PROPOSITION?

THE POTOSI TUNNEL.

See Illustration, preceding page, which gives a correct idea of its proportions and situation.

The Mines and Tunnel Property of the Potosi Mining and Smelting Company, who are just now enlarging their operations on a solid basis, with an outlook that is almost bewildering in its magnificent promise.

They own five of the principal mines of the district including the great Buena Vista, all of which are situated on the line of their tunnel, now in five hundred and twenty feet. They have in addition already cut two immensely valuable silver veins in the tunnel; one thirty feet between the walls, the other twelve feet, with three and one-half feet solid ore, assaying two hundred and forty eight dollars ($248.) per ton in silver, and eighteen per cent. lead.

From the vast outcrop of ore overlaying the line of the tunnel the company are warranted in expecting to find a lode every one hundred feet that is run in the tunnel.

PLAN OF WORKING.

With a Burleigh drill and air compressor of the largest size, driven by an engine of fifty horse power, capable of cutting in the slate and marble of the district ten feet per day, and of completing the tunnel to the Buena Vista ledge, the objective point, in eighteen months. Tunnel ten feet wide and eight feet high, with double track.

WHY CANNOT A RIVAL TUNNEL BE RUN?

Because the Potosi Company, by priority of location, and by occupying the only advantageous point f.om which a tunnel can be driven, possesses the exclusive ability to penetrate and work these vast bodies of ore. The Tunnel cuts the whole series of veins at an angle of sixty four degrees from three hundred to twenty-one hundred and forty feet deep, at an average depth of one thousand feet.

WHAT DOES THE COMPANY PROPOSE TO DO?

Push their Tunnel with the Burleigh drill ninety days. This

will bring them upon the lead deposits. Then in addition to tunneling, to put up a smelting furnace, take out their lead ores and silver ores, and reduce them, and increase the number of furnaces as fast as practicable.

The cost of a furnace will not exceed ten thousand dollars. What it can accomplish is shown by the following exhibit:

ESTIMATE POTOSI ORES.

Average assay Galena ores,.............$ 60.00 per ton in silver.
   "   "   Silver   " .... 100.00 " "

Furnace 30 tons capacity at Potosi dump.

EXPENSES.

Mining 30 tons,	@ $ 4.00	$120.00
Wood, 2 cords,	" 8.00	16.00
Charcoal, 7½ tons	" 38.00	285.00
Supt. and Labor		82.00
Freight, 10 tons, via R. R.	" 30.00	300.00
Refining 10 tons,	" 25.00	250.00
Repairs and Contingent Expenses per day,		25.00
Total Expense,		$1,078.00

RETURNS.

27 tons,	@ $ 60.00	$1,620.00	
3 "	" 100.00	300.00	
10 " Lead "	80.00	800.00	
			$2,720.00
Net Profit per day,			$1,642.00
" " " year, 300 days,			$492,600.00
Net Product per year, of 12 Furnaces,			$5,911,200.00

This estimate is based on the actual experience of the business in the district.

One furnace will consume only thirty tons of ore daily. One years work on the Tunnel will provide sufficient ore to run twelve furnaces.

WHAT OTHER ADVANTAGES DOES THE COMPANY POSSESS?

They will transport the ore of all the mines on the line of the Tunnel.

The other companys not having proper shafts and hoisting works, can well afford to pay a handsome royalty for the privilege of working their mines through the Potosi Tunnel and carrying their ores in its cars.

Five hundred thousand dollars ($500,000) per annum would be a moderate estimate of the revenue of the company from this source alone.

The Potosi Company will have the WATER TRADE of the district, and water is worth three cents per gallon on the average. Their tunnel will tap the water belt lower than the present source of of supply. There is already a very considerable flow of water in the tunnel. Within two years time their water ought to bring the Company a revenue of fifty thousand dollars ($50,000) per annum.

They have fire clay of the very best description, right at the mouth of the tunnel. To make fire brick, all that is requisite is to pulverize the clay, mix with quartz, mould to the proper shape for the furnace, sun dry it, and it is done. The necessary excavations for their furnace sites will be in beds of fire clay.

The principal owners and the Trustees of the Company are men of much experience in mining. Some of them have been intimately connected with the mining and smelting operations of this district for years. They have located their ground and laid their plans understandingly. They know whereof they affirm, when they say that there is no richer mining district in these United States than Cerro Gordo, and that the Potosi Company occupy the controlling position in this district.

The Capital Stock of the Potosi Mining and Smelting Co. is Five Million Dollars ($5,000,000.) divided into 50,000 shares of one hundred dollars ($100) each.

The Trustees of this Company are as follows:

JAMES A. PRITCHARD,   THOMAS HARDY,   HENRY RAYMOND,
   JOHN SIMPSON,   JAMES BRADY.

The officers are:

JAMES A. PRITCHARD,
President and Treasurer.

JACOB HARDY,
Secretary.

Office of the President: Rooms 1 and 2 Academy Building.

Secretary's office: 408 California Street, Room 2, San Francisco.

CALISTOGA SILVER MINES.

Napa Co., California.

In the spring of 1873, a large and well defined ledge of high grade silver bearing quartz was discovered on the easterly slope of Mt. St. Helena, in Napa County, and about six miles north of Calistoga.

ORGANIZING OF COMPANY, AND PROGRESS OF THE MINE.

Archie Borland, Coll Deane, Thos. R. Hayes and Alex Badlam organized a company and built one of the most perfect ten stamp quartz mills in the State, and in the fall of 1874 commenced to crush ore from the mine.

The pulp assays average about seventy-five dollars ($75.) and by the time the winter rains set in, about forty thousand dollars ($40,000.) in bullion had been shipped to San Francisco.

The bars contained about one-third gold, and two-thirds silver in valuation, and in fineness, an average of 990-1000ths,

In April of 1875, the mill again started, and the shipments of bullion again commenced.

About sixty thousand dollars ($60,000) has been spent in the development of the mines belonging to the Calistoga Silver Mining Co., which has been more than fully realized by the Co. from the bullion.

This Company have three thousand feet on the main ledge, which extends for miles, cropping out boldly in many places.

A large number of mines are being opened in this vicinity, and a lively little town has sprung up near the toll gate at the summit, called "Silverado."

The wonderful development of auriferous quartz of Mount St. Helena, and the successful and continuous working of the mine, explodes the oft repeated statement that "gold and silver in paying quantities, do not exist in the coast range."

www.ingramcontent.com/pod-product-compliance
Lightning Source LLC
Chambersburg PA
CBHW020300090426
42735CB00009B/1156